Amritam Gamaya

Lead Us to Immortality

Part 1

Amritam Gamaya

Lead Us to Immortality

Part 1

Śrī Mātā Amṛtānandamayī Dēvī

Translated by Rajani Menon

Mata Amritanandamayi Center, San Ramon
California, United States

Amritam Gamaya

Lead Us to Immortality

Part 1

Śrī Mātā Amṛtānandamayī Dēvī
Translated by Rajani Menon

Published by:
Mata Amritanandamayi Center
P.O. Box 613
San Ramon, CA 94583-0613, USA

In USA:
www.amma.org

In Europe:
www.amma-europe.org

In India:
www.amritapuri.org
inform@amritapuri.org

Contents

Preface

Like the gold in gold ornaments, the water in waves, and the clay in earthenware, spirituality is the very ground of life in all its manifestations. Such is Amma's vision. For her, spirituality is not only in the mainstream of life, it is the very riverbed on which the current of existence flows, swirls and eddies.

Amma's all-encompassing perspective is reflected in this book, a compilation of 108 messages on a wide range of topics. They include ethics and moral consciousness, the harmonizing of spirituality with material progress, the relevance of rituals and traditions, meditation and mind management, attentiveness and efficient action, the balance of head and heart, conflict resolution, love and compassion, the importance of living in the present moment, the necessity of a Guru, the bond between spouses, the role of spirituality in science, and so much more.

The sheer sweep of Amma's outlook is not only panoramic, it also reveals the perennial relevance of spirituality. As she says, "Spirituality is the management of life. It teaches us how to live in this world and how to overcome challenges."

The beauty of Amma's teachings, backed by the authority of insight and experience, lies in their simplicity and clarity. She thus makes timeless wisdom accessible to all. If we can take the advice she dispenses to heart, we can deepen our self-understanding and make our lives meaningful. Amma affirms that "Spirituality gives us an understanding of who and what we really are. This understanding makes us aware of our responsibilities, and we will then live in such a way as to benefit both ourselves and the world."

We pray that this book sheds the light of understanding in the lives of our dear readers and that it paves the way to a more auspicious future for them.

Publisher

1. Dharma

Children, *dharma* is what preserves the intrinsic nature of an object. The dharma of a lamp is to shed light, that of the eyes is to see, and that of the heart is to pump blood throughout the body. It is only when each organ in the body acts according to its dharma that we can lead healthy lives. Similarly, the universe can maintain its harmony only if all living beings follow their dharma properly. The sages of Bhārat (India) called the principle that sustains the harmony of the universe 'dharma.'

One can travel safely only if the vehicles on the road obey traffic rules. Similarly, it is only when each individual carries out his dharma sincerely that society can prevail and progress. The country can progress only if each citizen lives a life rooted in dharma. This is just as true for the family also. Peace and prosperity will prevail in the family only when each member lives honestly and behaves considerately.

A teacher must discharge his duties when he goes to school. However, his dharma at home is different. He must be a father to his children and a brother to his siblings. Therefore, one's dharma varies according to place and circumstance. Dharma is doing the right thing at the right time in the right way.

That said, we all have a dharma that is higher than all other dharmas, our *parama-dharma* (highest dharma): to realize the perfection within. Suppose a butterfly lays its eggs on a leaf. If an egg is destroyed, the purpose of its life will not be fulfilled; the same is the case if it dies during the larva or pupa stage. It attains the supreme goal of its life and fulfils its purpose only when it has metamorphosed into a butterfly and its beauty and innate talents have become fully manifest.

There is divinity in each and every one of us. That is our true nature. To realize this is the parama-dharma of every human being. Realization does not refer only to one's own salvation, but to a state in which one sees oneself in everyone. However, today, we are unable to understand the true value of the wealth that life is. We squander life away on trifling pleasures.

We must overcome this tendency. We must live with discernment and right knowledge. We must see God in ourselves as well as in every animate and inanimate being in this universe and thus fulfil our life.

2. Devotion and Humility

Children, where there is devotion, there will also be qualities like humility, patience and compassion. A real devotee sees himself as the servant of all, not as someone great. He is ready to help others, disregarding his own problems.

King Ambarīṣa, a staunch devotee of Lord Viṣṇu, observed the *Ēkādaśī* fast[1] without fail. Pleased with his devotion, Lord Viṣṇu bestowed on him the *Sudarśana Cakra.*[2] Seeing how devoutly Ambarīṣa observed the vow, Indra feared that he would lose his position as chief of the gods to the king. He incited Sage Durvāsa to call upon Ambarīṣa at his palace on an Ēkādaśī day in order to break the king's fast. The king greeted the sage with utmost reverence. Saying that he would first take a bath, Durvāsa went down to the river but did not return even when the time for breaking the fast was drawing near. So Ambarīṣa offered oblations to the gods, setting some aside for Durvāsa. Then, taking a sip of water, he broke his fast.

When Durvāsa returned from his bath and learnt that the king had ended his fast without waiting for him, he became enraged. He started verbally abusing Ambarīṣa, who remained unperturbed. Though aware of his own might, he contritely said again and again, "Please forgive me for any mistake I might have committed." But Durvāsa did not forgive him. He conjured

[1] A fast observed during the 11th lunar day of each of the two lunar phases that occur in a Hindu month.

[2] Literally, the 'disk of auspicious vision,' a spinning disk with serrated edges; Lord Viṣṇu's weapon.

a devil to slay Ambarīṣa. When the devil lunged forward to kill the king, the Sudarśana Cakra materialized and dispatched the fiend. It then hurtled towards Durvāsa's throat. The sage fled for his life. He sought refuge with Lords Brahma and Śiva but was unable to shake off the terrifying Sudarśana Cakra. Finally, he ran to Vaikuṇṭha, the abode of Lord Viṣṇu, where the Lord told him that his only recourse for salvation was Ambarīṣa's protection. Seeing no other way, Durvāsa ran to Ambarīṣa and begged forgiveness. Even then, such was the king's humility that he wanted to wash the sage's feet and drink that water.

God will always be with people like Ambarīṣa. He will always watch over and protect the humble. In contrast, how can one who feels "I am great; everyone must serve me" ever realize God?

There are some who, even while praying, brood revenge on others. An oxidized vessel cannot be plated with lead. It must first be scrubbed clean of its patina. Similarly, only when the heart is purified will devotion take root. Only then can we realize the presence of God within us.

3. Practicality of Devotion

Children, people criticize devotion and spirituality as blind faith, as mental weakness, and as a means of exploitation. Devotion is not blind faith. On the contrary, it is faith that removes blindness. Devotion is a practical science. It fosters righteousness in society, and offers relief from the sorrows of life. Faith in God gives one the strength to remain standing amidst the hard knocks of life. When we worship God, we assimilate his divine qualities. How many people have been uplifted by their faith in God!

We obey the words of one we love dearly. Suppose the girl we love says, "If you love me, you will stop smoking." If the boyfriend loves her sincerely, he will quit smoking at once. This is true love. Love has driven many to give up their bad habits. "I quit because she doesn't like me drinking." One might ask if this is not a weakness. Considering the benefits, it is certainly not a weakness but a strength.

Faith and devotion stop one from doing wrong and inspire us to do good. The presence of traffic rules minimizes road accidents. The presence of police and courts checks the incidence of crime. Similarly, devotion and spirituality are practical means of maintaining harmony in society. Through them, moral and ethical values become ingrained in people.

The path of devotion stresses an individual's responsibilities to society. Devotion to God and compassion towards fellow beings and the poor are like the two sides of a coin; if there is one, there will be the other. The compassion we show the poor is true worship of God. True devotion inspires us to give up the desire for inordinate wealth and to serve the poor with the wealth that is in excess of our needs. Pilgrims to Śabarimala undergo a ceremony during which they keep the *irumuḍi keṭṭu*[3] on their head. During this ceremony, it is customary to give coins to children. After performing the *hōma* (fire ritual) and other *pūjās* (forms of ritual worship), it is also customary to feed the poor and give them clothes and money. Thus, devotion nurtures civic consciousness and compassion. Similarly, snake worship and other pūjās for the protection of sacred groves protect and preserve the environment.

What we need is practical logic, not intellectual gymnastics. We tell children that if they lie, they will become blind. Though it is not true, doesn't this harmless lie guide them to the right path? We might not be able to see the logic behind certain customs that nevertheless confer many benefits to people. Such customs reach out to and uplift people.

There may be some who use devotion and spirituality to exploit others. Don't counterfeit coins come into existence because genuine coins have value? Just because there are two vulgar books in a library does not mean that the entire library is stocked with such books, does it?

Love and faith are the greatest gifts man has received. A life without them is like a painted corpse, i.e. lifeless. This does not mean that logic and intelligence are not needed; they are, but they have their place. Don't both the scissors, which cuts a cloth into pieces, and the needle, which sews them together, have their own uses? The question is not whether or not God exists but whether man suffers. We must think of practical ways in which we can mitigate the suffering. Devotion is the means of

---

[3] A small bundle with two pouches, the contents of which are to be offered to the Lord.

finding the solution to one's sorrow within oneself. Its relevance and usefulness will always prevail.

4. Bhaya-bhakti

Children, some people ask if fear has any place in the path of devotion, and if *bhaya-bhakti* (devotion accompanied by fear) is unhealthy. Amma would not say that bhaya-bhakti is unhealthy. Though there is no place for fear in the fullness of devotion, bhaya-bhakti certainly helps a beginner progress on the path of devotion. The Lord of the Universe dispenses the fruit of every action to every being. He protects the virtuous and punishes the wicked. The devotion of one who knows that God punishes evil deeds will contain both reverence and a slight tinge of fear. This fear will kindle discernment in him, thus enabling him to keep away from wrongdoing, and give him the strength to walk the right path.

Bhaya-bhakti is not like the fear a slave has towards his master; it encompasses not only fear but also a student's respect for his teacher, and a child's innocent love for his mother. Such ought to be our attitude towards God.

A child loves his mother and knows that she is his protector. At the same time, he also knows that if he does some mischief, his mother will not hesitate to punish him. Therefore, his love for his mother is tinged with fear. It is this fear that saves him from many dangers and misdeeds. A child's whims and fancies can tempt him to do wrong. However, fearing scolding and punishment from his mother, he steers clear of trouble. Thus, fear of his mother awakens discernment in him and prods him to walk along the right path. At the same time, this fear never hinders his love for his mother. On the contrary, it fosters healthy spiritual growth.

Children often study well when they are young because of fear of punishment from the teacher. This fear helps them overcome laziness and acquire knowledge. By the time they reach the higher grades, they are no longer dogged by such fear as they would have gained the necessary discernment by then. They will have only reverence and obedience to the teacher. Most devotees have such an attitude towards God.

As the devotee progresses on the path of devotion, bhaya-bhakti evolves to *prēma-bhakti* (loving devotion). In prēma-bhakti, there is not even the slightest trace of fear. Out of love for the Lord, the devotee receives even punishments from God joyfully. All the latent tendencies that incite him to doing wrong are washed away by the fervor of his devotion. A true devotee forgets everything else and becomes like a baby resting in the lap of his loving mother.

5. Rituals and Traditions

Children, the number of people who believe in God is increasing in our country. More and more people are going to places of worship. However, there does not seem to be a corresponding increase in spiritual awareness being reflected in their daily lives. In fact, there seems to be a degradation of values as well as increasing corruption and attachment to sensual pleasures.

Our religious consciousness seems to be associated largely with rituals and traditions. Generally, most people do not seem to have understood and assimilated spiritual principles properly; nor do they show much awareness of values. Even the knowledge that is propagated in places of worship seems to be focused more on promoting sectarianism than on increasing awareness of values. Thousands are ready to die for their religion but few are willing to live by spiritual principles and values. This is the main reason for the degradation of values in society.

Most devotees lack any real knowledge of the fundamental principles of religion. Many just blindly follow the religious practices of their ancestors. Once, the supervisor of a garden called four of his workers and gave them a job each: the first was to dig holes, the second, to sow seeds in them, the third, to water the seeds, and the fourth, to cover the holes with earth. They started working. The first worker dug holes. The second worker came late. Ignoring this, the third worker watered the holes, and the fourth worker covered them. All their efforts were in vain. The aim was to sow seeds and to grow seedlings but the second worker did not sow the seeds in the first place! Many religious people are like this. They go through the rigmarole of rituals but do not strive to assimilate spiritual principles and apply them. So, even though the numbers of believers have increased, society does not seem to have reaped the benefits of devotion.

The main aim of traditions and rituals is to cultivate remembrance of God and to inculcate noble values. Customs help to foster good habits. Following customs brings about discipline and order in life. That said, we must first strive to understand the spiritual principles behind the customs.

For as long as we are identified with the body, we need traditions and rituals. It is not enough just to say that everything is God or Brahman, the Supreme. We have not experienced this truth. Just as pictures and counting beads are used as aids to help teach children how to count, traditions and rituals are necessary to shape the mind.

It makes no difference to God whether or not we observe traditions and rituals. However, we need them for our inner growth. Traditions and rituals uphold noble values and protect the well-being of society. Without them, *dharma* (righteousness) itself will disappear.

6. Iṣṭa-dēvatā

Children, there are different conceptions of God in different religions. In truth, God has no name or form. He is devoid of form or attributes. However, it is not easy to worship the formless and attribute-less God. In order to cultivate devotion and concentration, we must turn to some form of God. Every devotee has the right to worship a form of divinity that he or she likes. This is *iṣṭa-dēvatā upāsanā*, worship of the form of God one likes.

Like the ocean tide that rises because of the moon's gravitational pull, God assumes many forms in response to the devotee's ardent desire. If God is conceived of as Lord Śiva, He will appear in that form. If God is worshipped as Dēvī, He will manifest as the Goddess. We can imagine any form, but we must have faith in that form. If we worship our iṣṭa-dēvatā with the attitude that he or she is the Supreme Self, our worship will culminate in a vision of the Self. Form is a ladder. Just as shadows disappear at noon, the form merges into the formless when concentration ripens in meditation.

Instead of worshipping different deities, we must worship our iṣṭa-dēvatā, regarding him or her as the Supreme. We must regard other forms of God as different aspects of our iṣṭa-dēvatā. If we worship different deities at different times, we will not gain the fruits of our worship so soon. Our mind must become established in the form of and mantra associated with our iṣṭa-dēvatā. If we are trying to dig a well, there is no point in digging small holes in many different places. We will find water only if we dig deep in one place. We must worship our one iṣṭa-dēvatā exclusively, regarding him or her to be the Supreme. This spiritual principle is reflected in the practice of Śabarimala pilgrims calling out, *"Swāmiyē Śaraṇam Ayyappa!"* ("Grant us refuge, O Lord Ayyappa!") no matter which temple they visit.

Only if we love our iṣṭa-dēvatā will his or her form become clear in our heart. We must pray constantly for a vision of our beloved deity. A devotee's attitude to God ought to be the same as that of a lover for his beloved. If he has seen his beloved in a blue sari, every time he sees the blue color, he will be reminded of her. Whether asleep or awake, he will be thinking of her alone. From the moment he wakes up, his mind will dwell solely on her. While brushing his teeth or sipping on his coffee, he will be thinking about what she is doing at this moment. We must have this same absorbing and all-consuming love for our iṣṭa-dēvatā. We must become incapable of thinking of anyone or anything other than our iṣṭa-dēvatā.

Even bitter gourd loses its natural bitterness and becomes sweet if immersed in sugar syrup for a long time. Similarly, by constantly meditating on and remembering his iṣṭa-dēvatā, the devotee becomes one with God.

7. Humility

Children, humility is the very first quality we ought to cultivate. Only one who is humble can receive God's grace. We should be humble in look, word and action. In India, we can see the carpenter touching his chisel reverentially before starting work, or musicians bowing down to their musical instruments before playing them. The ancient sages bequeathed to us a culture that taught us to revere everything. They thus aimed to destroy the ego in us.

While performing any action, we must not allow the thought that "I am doing it" to arise. We must cultivate the awareness that we are able to act purely by the strength that God has lent us. We must come to regard work as worship. Humility and simplicity draw God's grace.

Once, there lived a *mahātmā* (spiritually illumined soul) who was exceedingly humble. No matter what happened, he remained humble, accepting both praise and abuse with humility. One day, a *dēvatā* (celestial being) appeared before him and said, "I am pleased with your humility. I shall give you a boon. What would you like?"

The mahātmā declined the offer, but when the dēvatā insisted, he said, "Unbeknown to me, may every one of my actions become a blessing to the world."

"Let it be so," the dēvatā said and vanished.

From that day onwards, whatever his shadow fell on—including the land and all its beings, moving and unmoving—became blessed. The parched lands he walked through turned green. Withered trees and wilted plants revived and became heavily laden with blossoms and fruit. Wayside streams became filled with pure, fresh water. His presence revived the strength and spirits of the weary. It gave solace to grieving mothers and infused joy in the hearts of young children. The mahātmā, unaware of this, continued his life as an ordinary man.

There is humility within us. It is our true nature. But we have never before tried to awaken it consciously. If we are still reluctant to behave humbly, nature will force us to do so. As we undergo bitter experiences in life, we will naturally learn to behave humbly.

No matter how many noble qualities a person has, none of them will shine through if he lacks humility. Conversely, if he is humble, he will be well liked by everyone even if he has many shortcomings. Like water flowing down to the valley, God's grace will flow to him.

8. Ego, the Evilest Enemy

Children, our most evil enemy is the ego. It makes us inhuman. Most people believe that achievements are built upon the foundation of the ego. Perhaps people in the working world might feel that the ego cannot be effaced totally. That said, we should see to it that we keep the ego under control. No matter where one works, one must learn to handle the egoistic 'I' sense with maturity. If not, it will harm both the individual and society.

Consider a family. If its head cannot defer to the other family members or respect the opinions of his wife and children, will there be any peace and happiness at home? No, there will only be conflict, contention and a lack of consensus in that tiny world of three or four people.

Whether in business, politics or any other field, the biggest problem is hostile competition among those working in that field. The root cause of this problem is the unchecked ego. Such antagonism is common among members of the same political party, between rival parties, and among business associates. An individual or a few people engage in a tug of war to gain dominion over the others. In such situations, we can see some people mercilessly tormenting their opponents tactically, psychologically or even physically in a bid to flaunt how powerful they are. They will stoop to any means to prove this. They become insensible to the pains and sorrows of others. When we can see and think only through the tiny perspective of 'me and mine,' we lose our ability to forbear, forgive and sympathize. Once we become fixated on getting something at any cost, we will have no qualms in hurting others for personal gain.

Amma remembers a story. A man visited his lawyer to discuss matters pertaining to a case. He had misgivings about how it was unfolding. He told his lawyer, "I don't think I will win this case. You must find some way to win it." After a pause, he said, "I understand that the judge presiding over my case is crazy about cricket. I was thinking, what if we bought him a business-class ticket to watch the India-Australia match in Australia?"

When he heard this, the lawyer said "The judge prides himself on his honesty and impartiality. He can never be bribed. If we tried something like that, he will be furious and turn against you in indignation. You can imagine how the case will end."

The judge ruled in favor of the man. To celebrate the victory, he took his lawyer out for a meal. The lawyer said, "How do you feel now? What if you had sent him a free ticket to watch the cricket match in Australia? Can you imagine what the verdict would have been?"

The man said, "Oh, I was just about to tell you about it. I am immensely grateful for your valuable advice. In fact, I did send the judge a free ticket, but I sent it in my adversary's name!"

Children, such vile acts push us deeper into the dark trenches of the ego. It harms both us and society. Above all, we sacrifice our own integrity.

The ego is like a jail. One who has no control over the ego can never enjoy the joy and peace of freedom. Such a person might have material wealth and prosperity but will have no peace of mind or contentment, for he will be thinking only of himself and what he can get. The mind of such a person is like a prison cell. True freedom is liberation from the ego. Only spirituality can give us this freedom.

Contemplating spiritual principles is not contradictory to the gaining of material prosperity. One who is truly walking the spiritual path will unfailingly discharge his duty towards society and other people even while striving for material gains. More than just thoughts of 'me and mine,' such people will seek to understand the pains and sorrows of others and strive to express love and compassion towards them. They will take upon themselves the responsibility of helping those in distress. Such people will not be enslaved by the ego. They will try sincerely to overcome the ego's limitations.

Children, the ego is actually a burden. Once we realize this, it won't be difficult to put it down. Most people cannot see or understand that they have an ego. We hear people say "What an ego he has!" Instead, if we truly realize, "What an ego I have!" the ego will cease to be. Thereafter, we will experience true freedom.

9. Ego

Children, many people tell Amma, "I'm not able to laugh wholeheartedly. I'm unable to open up my heart when I speak, no matter whom I speak to. I'm always sad."

When we look around us, we will see that all creatures in nature, except man, live joyfully. Trees and plants sway blissfully in the breeze. Birds chirp without a care in the world. Rivers gurgle as they flow. There is bliss all around us. Why is man alone miserable though surrounded by so much joy?

Nature is not burdened with the weight of ego. It does not have the 'I' sense. Only human beings have egos. If we continue clinging to the ego, we will remain unhappy. If we abandon it, we will also be able to lead carefree and joyous lives.

As long as we retain the egoistic 'I' sense, we will not be able to find true strength within. If the curtains are closed, we will not be able to see the sky outside. But if we open the curtains, the sky will be visible. Similarly, we will behold our true self only if we get rid of the ego.

There was a sculptor who was mortally frightened of death. He tried to think of ways to escape death. Finally, he thought of a way. He sculpted 12 life-sized and life-like statues of himself. When death drew near, he stood among the statues. When the god of death came to take the sculptor's life away, he saw 13 identical figures. Unable to find the sculptor, the god of death stood thinking for a while. He then said to himself, "These statues are outstanding but there is a flaw in each one."

Hearing this, the sculptor jumped and shouted, “My statues? Flawed? What flaw?”

The god of death said, “This is the flaw,” and immediately seized the sculptor’s life.

When we think, “I am the doer,” misery arises. That very thought is bondage. Whether we are doing *pūjā* (ritual worship) or cleaning the drain, the thought “I am doing it” will defile the mind, and it will be difficult to cleanse such a mind. We must try to do everything as an offering to God. Only then will our mind become pure. Once we have boarded the bus, there is no need to continue carrying our baggage. We can put it down. Similarly, once we take refuge in God, we can offer the baggage of our ego to him and thus become free of sorrow.

10. Overcoming Weaknesses

Children, it is natural to make mistakes. There can be flaws in our behavior and actions. We might have character defects. But most people justify their actions when they make mistakes, stumble or fail. They try their best to cover up their failings. They might even argue that the mistake was not theirs but another person's. However, by blaming someone else, we can never overcome our failings. For example, the bitter experiences of childhood can leave indelible scars on the mind and even warp our character. Blaming our parents or others will not solve the problem. Our weaknesses might even become more pronounced and adversely affect our good relations with others.

A doctor examined a patient and said, "It'll be difficult to cure this disease completely as it is something you've inherited."

The patient interrupted the doctor at once: "If that's the case, please send the bill for the medical treatment to my parents!"

The man did not think about what he could do to control the disease. Instead, he held his parents accountable. He conveniently forgot the fact that by taking medicines, exercising regularly and controlling his diet, he could curb the disease. Many of us react like this patient when faced with our inadequacies and weaknesses.

It is because of our ego and false pride that we cover up our own mistakes and blame others. Hence, the ego must be conquered. If not, we will face defeat in both spiritual life and worldly matters. When we fail, we must turn inward and try to understand our weaknesses and inadequacies. Then, we must face them bravely. We must also make sincere efforts to overcome our weaknesses. Acknowledge our weaknesses, face them and overcome them—this is the progression.

We should not hide from or escape our own weaknesses by blaming others. If we have the openness of mind to assume responsibility for our failings and if we strive earnestly, we can overcome any weakness.

11. Remorse

Children, to err is human. There is no one who has done no wrong in life. Doing what one should not and not doing what one should—both are wrong. Some unknowingly make mistakes. Others make mistakes under the pressure of circumstances. Either way, the first step to correcting mistakes is to become aware of them.

Once we realize our mistake, we must repent. Repentance is a form of atonement. There is no sin that cannot be washed away by the tears of remorse. That said, once we know what is right, we ought not to repeat our mistakes. We must repent sincerely. Some people only pretend to be remorseful in front of others.

A young lad became a pickpocket. His bad habit sorely distressed his mother, who asked her son to confess his sin to the priest in a nearby temple and to beg for forgiveness. The day after he picked a businessman's pocket, the lad went to the priest and said, "O priest, I sinned yesterday. I stole a businessman's wallet."

Hearing this, the priest said, "You committed a terrible crime. Find the businessman at once and return his wallet!"

The boy found the businessman, returned the wallet, and went back home. That night, the mother saw her son counting money from a thick wad of notes. When she asked how he had obtained so much money, the son said, "I swiped money from the till near the priest when I went to confess my crime."

Our remorse should not be like this. It must be sincere.

Once we realize our mistake, we must resolve firmly to make amends and never repeat the mistake again. Whenever we do wrong, our conscience gently murmurs, "Do not do this! Desist!" If we listen to our conscience, we will not do wrong.

Sometimes, we do wrong out of ignorance. God will pardon such sins. However, if we keep repeating the same mistakes, He will not forgive us. Therefore, we must not repeat our mistakes.

Human life is a journey from error to truth. Though mistakes can happen, we must strive to correct ourselves. We must try to make our every thought, word and deed noble. Even if we make a small mistake, we must repent and correct it. This is the sole means to our ultimate victory, to eternal joy and peace.

12. The Road to Peace

Children, all of us want peace and happiness. Yet, we often face sorrow, frustration and disappointment. Why do we not have peace and happiness?

If we want to enjoy peace and happiness, we must first have a correct understanding of life. No matter how much money a rich man has, it will be of no use if he does not even know about his own wealth. Similarly, as long as we are unaware of our true nature, we will not be able to live in harmony with the world and discharge our *dharma* (duties in life) properly.

A group of travelers were walking to a distant village. After some time, they came to a forest. There was a pond nearby. Putting their belongings down on the bank, they went for a swim. When they returned, they found all their belongings missing. Thieves had stolen everything! The travelers set out at once in hot pursuit of the thieves. On the way, they saw a man resting in the shade of tree; he was a *mahātmā* (spiritually illumined soul). The travelers asked him if he had seen the thieves passing that way. The mahātmā said, "You're upset that your belongings have been stolen. Reflect for a moment. Are the thieves, who are instrumental in robbing your happiness, inside or outside you? Do you want to recover what you lost, or do you want to gain wealth that you can never lose? Think about it!"

Seeing the wisdom in the mahātmā's words, the travelers became his disciples.

There is boundless wealth in each one of us. But because we are not aware of this, we roam around in search of happiness from objects of the world. Some struggle to gain wealth and power whereas others strive for name and fame. Both mistakenly believe that once they attain their ends, they will have peace and happiness. But happiness is not something one gains from objects. In fact, desires stand in the way of true happiness. This happiness will reveal itself only when the mind stops hankering after one thing or the other. This understanding must become clear in our hearts. This is the first step to peace and happiness.

The Self is the source of eternal bliss and peace. Not realizing this, some seek comfort in drink and drugs. By so doing, they not only ruin their own lives, they also hurt their families and society. Spirituality gives us an understanding of who and what we really are. This understanding makes us aware of our responsibilities, and we will then live in such a way as to benefit both ourselves and the world.

13. Sorrows of Life

Some people say, "For years, I have been visiting temples without fail, and yet, I am still poor and my sorrows have not left me. Sometimes, I even wonder why I should call out to God!"

Do we really rely on God? If we did, we would prosper both materially and spiritually. No *mahātmā* (spiritually illumined soul) has ever starved to death. The life of one who has surrendered to God will never be sorrowful. People might ask if Kucēla[4] did not suffer from poverty. This is not totally correct. He had no time to grieve as he was always immersed in thoughts of God! His innocent love for God gave him the strength to remain joyful even in the midst of crippling poverty. His surrender released him from a fate of poverty and drew prosperity into his life.

None of us go to temples just for the sake of having the Lord's darśan. Even when we stand before God, we tell him only worldly things. Our devotion is not pure and selfless; we pray only to fulfil desires. It is not that we should not have desires, but our love for God should surpass our interest in fulfilling these desires.

Once, Lord Kṛṣṇa was sitting by the banks of the Yamunā with the *gōpīs* (milkmaids), who were listening in rapture to his sweet utterances. He asked them, "What do you do when you encounter sorrows and difficulties?"

One gōpī said, "I will pray to you, O Lord, to remove my sorrows."

---

[4] A poor devotee of Lord Kṛṣṇa. As a result of the Lord's blessings, he became fabulously wealthy.

Another gōpī said, "I will pray to you, O Lord, to be always by my side. Even if the summer heat is scorching, one will not feel its intensity if there is a cool breeze blowing. Likewise, when the Lord is with me, none of the hardships of life will affect me."

Yet another gōpī said, "When sufferings come, I will pray to the Lord for strength to overcome them."

Rādhā was listening silently to these responses. The Lord asked her, "O Rādhā, why are you silent? How will you face suffering?"

"I will meditate on the Lord within. I will remember him in my heart."

"Don't you pray for anything?"

"When Your form shines brightly in my heart, where is there a place for sorrow? When light dawns, darkness is naturally dispelled. I have never found any need to pray for anything."

A true devotee never bothers about hardships in life. Completely surrendered to God, she remains without worry, like a child resting in her mother's lap.

14. Time, the Greatest Wealth.

Children, our most precious wealth is time. Even if we lose a million dollars, we might still be able to recover it, but we can never regain lost time. Many realize the value of time only in the last moments of their life.

Alexander the Great, who conquered the whole world, understood the value of time only when he was on his deathbed. Realizing that death could seize him at any moment, he told those around him, "If there is anyone who can lend me even a single breath, I am ready to give him half my kingdom as compensation. In a bid to conquer nations and amass wealth, I squandered precious time and health. I now realize that I cannot stave off death for a single moment even with all my wealth."

Only experience can teach us the value of time. If we truly understood the value of time, we would cherish every moment as if it were a priceless treasure.

Once, a man received a letter asking him to attend an interview for a job he had wanted for a very long time. In order to reach the city where the interview was being held, he had to take two connecting flights. There was a half-an-hour gap between the two flights. He went to an airport restaurant and had a snack, for which he was billed ₹500. Seeing the bill, the man said, "This is way too much! I did not eat so much." Seeing how upset he was, the cashier reduced the amount by a hundred rupees. But the man insisted that he would pay nothing more than ₹300. Faced with no other choice, the cashier finally relented. Feeling triumphant at his victory over the cashier, the man sauntered to the boarding gate, grinning all the way. When he reached the gate, he learnt that his connecting flight had taken off five minutes before. Caught up with petty bargaining, he had forgotten his goal, and thus missed the opportunity of getting the job he had been dreaming about for years.

Some people complain that time is not on their side. Time is always favorable but we do not befriend time. It is we who decide if time works for or against us. Not realizing this, we become slaves to circumstance. If we just sit and wait for good times to come, many good things will pass us by. Do not wait for a propitious time to do a good deed. If it is good, do it at once.

15. Freedom from Sorrow

Children, knowingly or unknowingly, we seek happiness through every action. We long to be free from all sorrow. However, our search may not be an informed or mindful one.

Every experience of sorrow carries a message. Suppose we accidentally touch a lighted stove and burn our hand while working in the kitchen. Suppose we did not feel pain. What would it be like? It is because we can feel pain that we are able to retract our hand at once from the stove. Likewise, the pain and sorrow that we suffer in daily life is a reminder that "it's time for a change!" Usually, we try to make external changes and this might give us a temporary reprieve from our sorrows. But if we wish to be free from sorrow once and for all, we must change our outlook and attitude radically.

A devotee used to visit a *mahātmā* (spiritually illumined soul) regularly and complain about the problems in his life. One day, when he started complaining, the mahātmā said, "Bring me a glass of water and a handful of salt." When the man brought those items, the mahātmā said, "Add half the salt into the water and stir well. Then drink the water and tell me how it tastes."

The devotee did as he was told and said, "It is too salty for consumption!"

The mahātmā then took him to a freshwater lake and said, "Drop the rest of the salt into this lake and then take a sip of the water."

The devotee took a sip and said that the water was fresh and pure. The mahātmā asked him, "Isn't the water salty?"

The devotee replied, "Not at all!"

The mahātmā then said, "Look, salt is like the sorrows of life, and fresh water, like our innate bliss. The water in the glass became undrinkable after you added just a little salt to it. But the same amount of salt made no difference to the freshness of the lake water. At present, your mind is as narrow as the glass. If you make it as expansive as the lake and awaken your inner happiness, then no sorrow can ever touch you."

Happiness is our natural state. But when we give undue importance to matters that create sorrow, our mind becomes fixated on them and we helplessly undergo sorrow.

Let the birds of sorrow fly over your head but never allow them to build a nest on it. Instead of brooding over problems all the time, engage yourself in creative work. Help others in whatever way possible. The mind will then become expansive. The heavy burden of sorrow will leave you and you will experience the bliss of the Self.

16. Selfless Service

Children, all religions give a lot of importance to selfless service. It purifies the mind and makes one worthy of God's grace. However, the service we render should be without any expectation. We should not expect even a word of thanks or appreciation. If we do, it will be like working for wages; such work will not help to purify the mind.

When we act without any desire for personal gain, selfishness leaves our heart, at least while we are working. Such work purifies the mind. However, if we engage in selfless service with an eye to gaining *puṇya* (spiritual merit), acknowledgement or remuneration, the very purpose of service becomes defeated.

Many donate to temples or churches with expectations of compliments or recognition. There are people who donate tube lights to temples and then paste printed messages such as 'Donated by so-and-so' on it, thus dimming its brightness. Such people want others to know about their donation and will be displeased if they are not at least thanked for it.

Once, a rich man went to pray in a temple. He gave a big donation to the priest, who neither thanked him nor lauded him for the donation. The rich man started saying, "I'm sure no one has ever donated such a huge sum of money to this temple before..."

The priest tolerated his self-glorification for some time. But when the donor did not look as if he was going to stop, the priest said, "Why brag like this? Do you expect me to thank you for your donation?"

"What's wrong with expecting at least a word of appreciation for the sum I donated?" the rich man asked.

The priest said, "You ought to be grateful that the temple accepted your donation. It is only a tiny fraction of God's wealth, which you are hoarding. You will receive his grace only if you can donate without pride. You ought to feel grateful that you have received an opportunity to serve God and his devotees. If you don't, it's best that you take the money back."

It is the mind that must be surrendered to God. Offering to him what the mind is attached to is akin to offering the mind itself. In truth, nothing belongs to us; everything belongs to God. We must be grateful to him for giving us the ability and opportunity to serve. When we understand that even our body, mind and intellect are gifts from God, we will become free of pride and selfishness. When we become free of pride, we become deserving of God's grace.

17. Stillness of the Mind

Children, the mind is a flow of thoughts. There is never a moment when the mind stops thinking. At times, the flow of traffic on the roads will be fast and furious, or, at other times, slow and leisurely. But it is not so with thoughts. Often, the flow of thoughts does not abate even in sleep. It is the mind's nature to brood over the past and to fret about the future.

Once, a middle-aged man was traveling in a train. A young man sitting beside him asked, "What's the time?"

Hearing this, the man said, "Shut up!"

Another passenger witnessing this interaction asked, "He only asked you for the time. Why do you need to get so angry over such a simple request?"

The man replied, "Yes, he asked only for the time. Suppose I tell him the time. He will start talking about the weather. He will then talk about the headlines in today's newspaper. He will talk politics next. Then he will ask about my family. I might then inquire about his family as well. Having thus become acquainted with each other, I might invite him home after disembarking. He might even spend a night there. I have a beautiful daughter, who might fall in love with him. Or he might fall in love with her. I shall never agree to my daughter marrying a man who does not even own a watch. This is why I shut him up right at the start to avoid any further conversation."

If someone asks for the time, we can either tell him the time or keep quiet. Was there any need for this man to imagine so much of the future? Because of the conflict in his mind, the other passengers also lost their peace of mind.

If the mind says 'stop' while we are walking, our legs will stop moving immediately. If the mind says 'stop' while we are clapping, the hands will stop moving at once. However, if we tell the mind to stop, will it? No. That said, we should be able to stop the mind. This is why we practice meditation. Just as we use a remote control to turn the television and other electric appliances on and off, meditation can help us bring the mind under our control.

Above all, we need a still mind to realize our true nature. We can enjoy supreme bliss and peace only in that stillness. May my children be able to awaken to such a state.

18. Maturity

Children, while facing difficult situations in life, we rarely try to find out the real cause of the difficulties. But unless we do so, we will not be able to find a permanent solution to these problems. For example, if a child starts crying because of hunger, the mother will try to appease him by giving him toys. The child may get distracted for a while. But when his hunger pangs increase, he will start wailing even more loudly. He will stop crying only when his hunger is appeased.

Some people turn to drugs and drink to forget their problems. Not only do these intoxicants not solve any problem, they also ruin one's health and wealth, and rupture family ties.

Once, two friends were talking to each other. One of them asked the other, "I heard that you started drinking. Why?"

His friend replied, "I'm facing many problems now and am trying to drown my sorrows in drink."

"So, did you succeed in drowning your sorrows?"

"No, my friend. My problems have learnt to swim in the alcohol!"

The root cause of all our problems is our headstrong desire to have everything go our way, according to our likes and dislikes. This willfulness is the source of all our negativities, including anger, hatred and jealousy. Willfulness is like a computer virus that wipes out all its data. It undermines our sense of discernment and destroys our peace of mind. We lose control over ourselves.

We cannot change the world according to our whims and fancies. Instead, we must learn to adjust to the situation and respond discerningly. We must learn to accept what we cannot change. A fragrant rose is surrounded by prickly thorns. To insist that a rose bush have no thorns but only flowers is impractical. Night always follows day. If there is joy, there will be sorrow. We must accept both. A tortoise can never behave like an elephant. Similarly, an elephant can never be a tortoise. See each for what it is and accept a tortoise as a tortoise and an elephant as an elephant. Do not leap for the skies in happiness, and do not collapse in sorrow. Remain content and joyful under any situation. The ability to do so is what we mean by maturity.

The mind becomes mature only when one stops being willful. A mature mind can face problems wisely. It is the ultimate solution to all the problems in life.

19. True Friend

Children, change is the nature of life. Both good and bad things can happen in life without any warning. Nothing lasts forever in this world. Today's friend can be tomorrow's enemy. God is our only true friend. No matter how many relatives and or how much worldly wealth we may have, they can never give us lasting happiness. Therefore, we should cultivate an inner bond with God alone.

One waters the roots of the tree, not the branches. Only then will the water reach all parts of the tree. Similarly, by loving God, we love all of creation. Thus, we will not become enslaved by excessive attachment to anyone even while leading a family life.

Many of us know the story of the mud-ball and the dry leaf who played hide and seek. Though it is a story for children, it conveys a profound meaning. While the mud-ball and dry leaf were playing, suddenly, the wind started blowing. The mud-ball began to worry: "Oh no! The dry leaf will be blown away!" To save the dry leaf, the mud-ball sat on top of the leaf. After some time, it started raining. The dry leaf covered the mud-ball to prevent it from being washed away. After a while, there was both rain and wind. What happened? The leaf was blown away and the mud-ball was washed away.

Our life is also like this. When we depend on others, small gains and victories might come our way. But no one will be able to help us in a major crisis. Our only refuge and saving grace then will be surrender to the divine. Only surrender ensures lasting peace and contentment in life.

This does not mean that we should not love our spouse or children or that we should regard them as strangers. We must love and protect them but must never forget that God is our only true friend. Everyone else will leave us sooner or later. Therefore, let us depend on God alone, considering all difficulties we face in life as fuel for our inner growth. If we do so, we can enjoy peace and happiness in family life also.

Depending on God does not mean that we won't face sorrow or difficulty in life. We will, but the difficulties will be greatly reduced. Not only that, even in the midst of difficulties, we will be able to retain our self-confidence and contentment.

It is enough to catch the queen bee; the other bees will follow her. Similarly, if we depend on God, both spiritual and material prosperity will come our way.

20. Lord Rāma

Children, God incarnates on earth when *adharma* (unrighteousness) flourishes and *dharma* (righteousness) declines, to reinstate dharma. Śrī Rāma, who was born thousands of years ago on the ninth day of the month of *Caitra* (March – April), is believed to be the very embodiment of dharma.

Avatars (incarnations of God) teach people by personal example. They reflect the limitations of the age they live in. Like everyone else, they, too, have to undergo trials and tribulations in life. They teach us not how to evade problems but how to live in their midst without compromising one's ideals and values. They show us how to face the trials of life with unruffled poise. Thus, their lives serve as an inspiration for us to follow the path of dharma.

Many people might wonder why, if Lord Rāma was all-knowing, he went after the golden deer. Did he not know that it was the demon Mārīca in disguise? It was then that Sītā was abducted. Lord Rāma assumed the human form with all its quirks and foibles. Therefore, like other human beings, he, too, manifested knowledge and ignorance, strength and weakness. Once you have started playing a game, you cannot change the rules of the game halfway through, can you?

Amma is reminded of a story. A prince was playing hide and seek with his friends in the palace garden. He forgot himself completely in the joy of the game. When it was his turn to find his friends, he ran around and searched in many places for a long time but could not find even one of them. An attendant watching all this asked him, "O Prince, why go through all this trouble to find your friends? Just order them, 'Come before me!' and they will come running to you at once, won't they? All you need to do is to exercise your authority and command them just once."

Hearing this, the young prince looked with pity at the attendant and said, "If I did so, what fun would there be in the game then?"

Just like other people, *mahātmās* (spiritually illumined souls) also face joys, sorrows, challenges, problems and limitations in their lives. They do so in order to allow others to draw closer to them and establish a personal bond with them.

In truth, avatars come with an aim that surpasses the safeguarding of dharma: they want to cultivate devotion in human hearts. They captivate people through their enchanting *līlās* (divine play). From childhood itself, we grow up, forging bonds with others. Our first bond is with our mother. We then establish ties with our father, siblings and others. It then becomes easy for us to connect to God in human form. This is how Śrī Rāma and Śrī Kṛṣṇa won a place for themselves in human hearts. Thus, through them, the culture of devotion flourishes in the world.

The ways in which Lord Rāma faced each and every situation in life are lessons for us to learn. His life teaches us how one ought to behave towards one's parents, siblings and friends, the ideal behavior of a king towards his subjects, and how to conduct oneself during moral crises. Śrī Rāma was not overly elated when he learnt that he was to be crowned king, nor did he become disheartened when the prospect of kingship was snatched away. He continued to behave lovingly and respectfully even towards Kaikēyī, who was instrumental in this change of fortune. Thus, in every way, Lord Rāma was an ideal exemplar of the noblest values that we ought to follow in life.

Advice to Lakṣmaṇa

The story of Śrī Rāma has been captivating and uplifting the hearts of millions of people for centuries. Mahātmās act with extraordinary presence of mind, courage and practical intelligence in circumstances that would confound ordinary people. They also reveal boundless compassion and endless patience. *Lakṣmaṇōpadēśa*, the advice Śrī Rāma gave Lakṣmaṇa, is one such instance.

When Rāma learnt that he was going to be exiled into the forest in order to honor his father Daśaratha's words, he prepared himself with utmost composure. He did not have any anger or resentment. There was not even the slightest twitch in his facial muscles. But Lakṣmaṇa, who saw and worshipped Rāma as God, started seething with uncontrollable rage and hatred towards Daśaratha and Kaikēyī, the very people sending Rāma away on the 14-year exile. Seeing this, Śrī Rāma lovingly caressed his beloved younger brother. His very touch calmed Lakṣmaṇa a little. Every word that Lord Rāma uttered thereafter and his every gesture were so adroit that they could have come from a master psychologist.

Every emotion produces unique vibrations. The vibrations of affection a mother has for her baby are different from those emanating from an angry man or a drunkard. The vibrations of lust are entirely different. Śrī Rāma had a placid and peaceful temperament. Therefore, it was no surprise that his presence and touch brought about a change in Lakṣmaṇa's mind.

Initially, Rāma did not give Lakṣmaṇa any spiritual advice; He knew that no advice can enter the mind of an angry man. One must calm him down at first. Only a calm mind can hear and understand. Instead of calling Lakṣmaṇa "Daśarathātmaja" ("son of Daśaratha"), Rāma addressed him as "Saumitra" ("son of Sumitrā"). Furious with his father and Kaikēyī for the injustice meted out towards his elder brother, Lakṣmaṇa had already unsheathed his sword. If Rāma had so much as mentioned Daśaratha's name then, Lakṣmaṇa's anger would have doubled! Rāma felt that by reminding him of his own mother, who was a repository of wisdom and maturity, Lakṣmaṇa's fury would abate. That is why he hailed him as "Saumitra."

Mahātmās do not just provide solutions to temporal problems. They use temporal troubles as a pretext for imparting eternal truths that can help solve the ultimate problems of life. Rāma adopted this approach in the advice he gave Lakṣmaṇa.

This was the same tactic Śrī Kṛṣṇa used with Arjuna, who had become petrified by the prospect of fighting the Kurukṣētra War. Through Lakṣmaṇa and Arjuna, Lords Rāma and Kṛṣṇa showed humankind the true way to peace and victory.

Rāma-rajya

Mankind has always dreamt of a society in which peace and prosperity prevail and where the ruler protects his citizens like his own children. That is why, even today, we remember Mahābalī's rule, where everyone was equal, and Rāma's reign (*Rāma-rajya*), when everyone was treated justly.

Rāma-rajya was marked by abundant prosperity. The king adhered to dharma, and his subjects followed suit. Rāma-rajya has become synonymous with ideal governance.

Once, there was an assembly of poets in the court of King Bhōja. A poet recited his poem, in which he extolled King Bhōja as an equal to Lord Rāma and his rule as utopian as Rāma-rajya. When he had finished his recital, everyone clapped. At that moment, a crow flew in and pooped on the head of the poet, who became upset. The king ordered the crow to be caught. The crow started speaking: "O King, I pooped on this poet's head because he lied. You are neither Rāma's equal nor is your reign equivalent to Rāma-rajya. I shall prove this to you. Please follow me."

The king, his ministers and the poet followed the crow. When they reached a cave, the crow went inside and asked them to start digging. Their excavation uncovered thousands of glittering gems. The crow said, "During Rāma-rajya, there was a wealthy man who had no children. He vowed to give the king a potful of jewels if he had a child. By God's grace, he soon became a father. He went with a vessel of jewels to Rāma, who declined the gift and asked him to distribute it instead among the poor in the kingdom. But there was not even one poor person during Rāma-rajya. Lord Rāma then asked the man to give the jewels to anyone who wanted them, but none was prepared to accept wealth that they had not earned through effort. These are the very jewels no one wanted."

The crow continued, "O king, order your ministers and the poet to open their palms!" When they did as told, the king saw jewels in their hands. The crow said "O king, I hope you have understood at least now that your kingdom is no Rāma-rajya!"

Though this story might sound far-fetched, it is nevertheless a beautiful depiction of ideal rule. A ruler has no friends or relatives, only subjects. Their well-being is his sole interest. For an ideal ruler, ruling is a form of austerity, a worship of the divine, a self-sacrifice for the sake of the world. Such was Rāma's rule.

Sītāyana

When we hear the word *Rāmāyaṇa*, the first person who comes to mind is Rāma. That said, Sītā is of equal importance. Her undying loyalty to Rāma, and her patience, forbearance and dedication to values are unparalleled. The Indian ideal of womanhood finds luminous expression in Sītā. The sanctity of family ties has been maintained over centuries because of her.

When Rāma tried to stop Sītā from following him into the forest, she reminded him that it was the right and responsibility of a wife to be by her husband in happiness and sorrow.

Her words are an eye opener in today's society, which avoids responsibilities and is intent on gains alone.

The abduction of Sītā reveals the glory of *viraha-bhakti*, devotion born of separation from God. Sītā hankered after the golden deer even when Rāma was with her. That is to say, her mind became enslaved by desire. But after Rāvaṇa abducted her, Sītā was constantly aching for Rāma. Like a blinkered horse looking at nothing other than the path before it, her mind was focused wholly on Rāma. When the moon (*candra*) shines, we notice the moon and not the darkness of the night. Similarly, in her distress, Sītā became focused entirely only on Rāmacandra, not on the gloom created by his absence. Rāvaṇa tried hard, in person and through messengers, to tempt Sītā. He promised to make her the Queen of Laṅkā and to hand over all his wealth to her if she accepted him. But Sītā remained unmoved. She bravely endured the unrelenting harassment and verbal abuse at the hands of the vicious demonesses. Even in the thick of such misery, Sītā was meditating on Rāma alone. In the suffering wrought by separation, all her *vāsanās* (latent tendencies) were sublimated. Finally, her heart was totally purified and she became reunited with Rāma.

Love becomes more intense when separated from one's lover. Such love has the frantic intensity of fish out of water gasping for air and struggling to get back into the water. We can see this attitude in Sītā and the *gōpīs* (milkmaids) of Vṛndāvan. From this, we see that a devotee who thinks constantly of God can mentally transcend any situation, no matter how challenging or painful.

When Hanumān expressed his desire to liberate Sītā from captivity and take her back to Lord Rāma, Sītā's response was telling: that if anyone other than Rāma saved her, it would tarnish his sterling reputation. This clearly shows that even amidst grave danger, Sītā remained broad-minded and poised.

Her life is a source of undying inspiration to devotees of God, and a beacon light for families. It is a sacred Ganges nourishing and purifying human hearts.

Devotion in the Rāmāyaṇa

Children, even after thousands of years, human hearts are still captivated by the *Rāmāyaṇa*. What is the secret of its appeal? It is the flavor of devotion that permeates the *Rāmāyaṇa*. This flavor softens and purifies human hearts. If bitter gourd is immersed in jaggery for many days, its natural bitterness will be transformed into sweetness. In the same way, if we direct our mind Godward and surrender to Him, it will become cleansed of all impurities.

One can see in the *Rāmāyaṇa* the diverse forms and moods of devotion. Lakṣmaṇa's devotion was different from Bharata's. Sītā's devotion was not the same as Śabarī's. Longing for proximity to and the presence of one's lover is one characteristic of devotion. We can see this quality in Lakṣmaṇa. He was ever engrossed in serving Rāma, even forgoing food and sleep. Bharata's devotion was different; it was serene. For him, ruling the kingdom was an act of worshipping Rāma. Any action becomes worship if we do it with remembrance of God and an attitude of surrender. If not, even temple worship becomes just another act.

Hanumān's devotion encompassed the qualities of discernment, enthusiasm, faith, trust and surrender. A minister of Sugrīva, Hanumān became Rāma's servant when he met the Lord. Whereas his relationship with Sugrīva was worldly, Hanumān's bond with Rāma personified the relationship between the *jīvātmā* (individual self) and *Paramātmā* (supreme self). Hanumān also shows how one can constantly think of the Lord through *japa* (repeated chanting of the Lord's name).

Devotion does not come from high birth or scholarship. Only a pure heart can gain devotion. This is what we can learn from Śabarī. When her Guru told her that Rāma would come to her one day, Śabarī trusted him completely. Every day, she would clean the āśram and keep the pūjā utensils ready in anticipation of his arrival. She would prepare a seat for him. Days, months and years passed. Her wait was not in vain. One day, Rāma reached Śabarī's āśram and accepted her hospitality. Her story proves that the Lord will definitely come to a heart that waits faithfully for him.

Devotion should not be merely emotional. Such devotion might be intense but is transient. What is needed is devotion rooted in knowledge. Devotion should not be for the sake of fulfilling some wish. After the seeds of devotion have sprouted, they must be transplanted in the fields of knowledge. We will then reap a good harvest and attain true knowledge.

Rāma was able to kindle devotion in his siblings, friends, subjects, birds and beasts. We unknowingly worship at the altar of greatness, wherever it is found, for the seed of devotion is hidden within each heart. We must nourish it through thought, word and deed. It must grow until we see that the whole universe is pervaded by divine consciousness. The *Rāmāyaṇa* shows us the way to this realization.

The Rāmāyaṇa Culture

Children, the values necessary for leading a noble life must be imparted to every child, and these values must be transmitted at home. The elderly must become role models for the young. They must give them moral lessons either through affectionate advice or stern admonishment. In the past, grandmothers and mothers used to tell Purāṇic stories to children, who would assimilate values from them. The *Rāmāyaṇa* is the most suitable means for imparting a noble culture and values to the younger generation.

Many characters in the *Rāmāyaṇa* demonstrated noble ideals in their lives, thus inspiring us to emulate them. Lakṣmaṇa was a repository of brotherly love and devotion to his elder brother.

Bharata was the personification of selfless love and self-sacrifice. Sītā demonstrated forbearance, determination and unflinching loyalty to her husband. Hanumān epitomized skill in action and total surrender. There are many such role models that children can choose.

Daśaratha did not go back on the word he had given Kaikēyī even though it broke his heart. What had drawn him to her was not her beauty and the love she showed him but her readiness to sacrifice her life for his in the battlefield. As for Rāma, he gave up the throne, as if it were an insignificant blade of grass, in order to uphold his father's pledge. What about Sītā? When Rāma decided to go to the forest, she could have said, "Don't go to the forest. This kingdom is your birthright." But she did not. Instead, she silently followed her husband to the forest. What did Bharata demonstrate? He did not think, "Now that my brother is out of the way, I can rule the kingdom without any hindrance!" Instead, he went in search of his brother, brought back his *pādukas* (sandals), which he placed reverentially on the throne, and ruled the country as a regent, eschewing all the comforts of royalty and adopting an ascetic lifestyle.

The characters in the *Rāmāyaṇa* demonstrated the ideals necessary for the well-being of any family. We must transmit these values to our children. However, we often fail in this regard, and this failure is reflected in today's society, which produces Kamsas.[5] In order to bring about a change and produce Rāmas and Hariścandras[6] instead, our homes must become imbued with the culture of the *Rāmāyaṇa*.

The *Rāmāyaṇa Kiḷippāṭṭu*[7] takes the form of advice that Lord Śiva, the head of the family, gave Pārvatī, the mother. We

---

[5] Kamsa was Lord Kṛṣṇa's uncle. He tried repeatedly to kill the Lord but was eventually killed by him.

[6] A legendary king known for adhering to truth at any cost.

[7] Popular Malayāḷam version of the *Rāmāyaṇa*.

should reclaim a culture in which parents converse about God and spiritual matters, and children grow up hearing such talk. Then, there will be love, unity and prosperity at home. Peace and values will dawn in society.

Devotion to Lord Rāma

Children, both the *Rāmāyaṇa* and *Mahābhārata* teach us how to overcome the obstacles of worldly life to attain the Supreme. We can learn from every character in the *Rāmāyaṇa*. It clearly shows how even noble characters can fall into disgrace as a result of thoughtlessness. Through their lives, we can understand the difference between good and bad, righteousness and unrighteousness.

Though there are many ideal characters in the *Rāmāyaṇa*, the most luminous one, by any reckoning, is Hanumān. He was not egoistic at all. He surrendered his body, mind and all his powers to Rāma. While striving to do Rāma's work, Hanumān even forgot the word 'rest.' It is believed that Hanumān lives on even today solely to chant the name of Rāma and to hear stories of the Lord.

An incident in the life of Hanumān illustrates the true nature of a Guru-disciple relationship. Once, when a sage had cupped some river water in his hand to perform the evening worship, a *gandharva* (celestial being) traveling in the skies looked down and spat. The spittle fell into the cupped hands of the sage. Upset and angry, he went to Śrī Rāma and asked him to kill the gandharva and thus redeem the wrong done to him. Rāma agreed to his request.

When the gandharva learnt about this, he sought refuge with Hanumān's mother. He tearfully begged her, "O Mother, I'm in grave danger. Please save me!"

His plea moved her motherly heart, and she told Hanumān, "O son, I have given the gandharva my word that I will save his life. You must fulfil my word."

Hanumān agreed. When Śrī Rāma came to kill the gandharva, Hanumān told the gandharva to stand behind him and chant Lord Rāma's name. Hanumān also joined his palms in prayer and chanted Rāma's name. All the arrows that Rāma shot at the gandharva were transformed into flowers that fell at the Lord's feet. Finally, Hanumān prayed to Rāma, "O Lord, if You permit, let the gandharva beg the sage for forgiveness." Both Śrī Rāma and the sage agreed to this proposal. Thus they reached an amicable solution and the gandharva was saved from mortal danger.

Even when Hanumān had to face Rāma in battle, he took refuge in the Lord and his name. Not only that, he led others to the path of devotion towards Rāma, thus demonstrating the supreme dharma of a disciple. Hanumān was the ideal disciple; we shall not find another like him.

21. Preconceived Notions

Children, knowingly or unknowingly, many of us harbor prejudices about others. Our preconceptions do not allow us to understand them properly. A man wearing yellow-tinted glasses will see everything as yellow. We must be ready to remove the spectacles of preconceived notions before looking at the world.

Even if we go to the same tailor regularly, he will take our measurements anew whenever we visit. A good tailor will never stitch new clothes using old measurements because he knows that our size might have changed since the last measurement. But we do not realize that our views about others might have also become obsolete. We must adopt the tailor's perspective in our daily life.

Many problems arise when our interactions with others are prejudiced. There is no reason why a thief cannot turn over a new leaf. Piṅgalā, a prostitute, became an ardent devotee. Ratnākaran, the notorious dacoit, was transformed into the venerable Sage Vālmīki. If we can interact with others without preconceptions, we can discover newness in the same individuals.

A case was being heard in court. The lawyers for both the plaintiff and defendant were arguing heatedly, but the judge was sitting with his eyes closed, not paying particular attention to either of them. After some time, he fell asleep. Seeing this, the clerk said, "Your Honor, you're falling asleep. You're not listening to either lawyer."

The judge retorted, "Don't worry. I've already decided the verdict!" He then went back to sleep.

If we behave like the judge in this story, i.e. with preconceived notions, justice and truth will be forfeited. A few individuals will receive undeserved concessions while a few others will face unjustifiable distress.

As a result of our own prejudices, we stand to lose those who could be our friends and helpers. Sometimes, these prejudices might even betray us.

Sometimes, we become the victims of our own prejudices. We might strongly believe that we cannot do certain things. However, we might actually be able to do it if we persevered. Such preconceptions reflect a lack of self-confidence, which is as dangerous as an inflated sense of our abilities.

Prejudices enslave us only because we give undue importance to the past. We must learn to live in the present moment always and strive to keep our heart and head free and efficient.

22. Drop Preconceived Notions

Children, if we examine how we respond to the situations we encounter, we will see that, most of the time, preconceived notions shape our responses. We must learn to regard the circumstances of our life without prejudice. We ought to be like the tailor, who takes measurements anew every time a customer wants something made. He will not make the clothing based on measurements taken previously. Knowing that one's size can change in a short span of time, the tailor will take fresh measurements every time. There is an important lesson here that we must learn: never assume anything.

Amma remembers a story. A middle-aged man was strolling with his young son in a park. The son excitedly asked, "Look, dad, isn't this a rose?"

With great joy and enthusiasm, the father replied, "Yes, son, it is."

"Is the color of this rose what they mean by red?"

"Yes, son, this is red."

Seeing the sprawling green lawn before him, the youth asked, "Dad, is this grass? Is this the green color?"

"Yes, son, this is grass and the color of grass is green."

In this way, father and son kept pointing at various things and talking in loud and excited voices. A man longing for some peace and quiet was sitting on a bench in the park. Enraged by the disturbance, he told the father, "People like me come here, hoping to enjoy some peace of mind, but because you and your son are talking so loudly, I have lost whatever peace I had. No matter what that mentally retarded kid says, you keep saying "Yes, son... yes, son." But that's not going to make him any better."

Hearing this, father and son remained silent for a while. Then, regaining his composure, the father said, "Forgive us. My son isn't retarded. He was born blind. Two days ago, he underwent a surgery to give him vision. After the bandages were removed, I wanted to take him to a place where he could see beautiful sights. That's why we came here. Enraptured by the beauty of this garden, which he was seeing for the first time, he asked me many questions excitedly, and I enthusiastically answered him, forgetting everything else. When one finds treasure, how joyful one will be! In that elation, one will even forget one's surroundings. That's how it was with us. Please forgive us."

Hearing this, the man felt remorseful. He begged forgiveness for having spoken such sharp words. On that day, he took a vow: "Henceforth, I will never judge anyone prematurely and get angry with him or her."

When he realized that his anger was caused by a misunderstanding and preconceived notions, the anger turned into love and compassion. If we can patiently gauge situations, we will definitely be able to awaken love and compassion in our hearts. May my children be able to do so.

23. Childlike Heart

Children, the rampant selfishness and egoism found in society today are smothering the tiny world of children's innocent play and laughter. At present, we are familiar only with cunning and artificial smiles, which are not really smiles, only a stretching of the lips. There is no sincerity behind them. We must reclaim the child's world, filled with innocent play and laughter. A child's heart is lying dormant within each one of us. Without awakening it, we can never experience peace or joy.

A child-like heart does not mean childishness, which refers to indiscriminate and immature behavior. A child-like heart is different; it refers to the attitude of a beginner, the curiosity and enthusiasm to learn about everything without becoming bored. There is wisdom in a child-like heart. Some might say that a child has no discernment. But he is wise enough to know that he can depend on no one but his mother.

A child plays with abandon, enjoying himself and forgetting the world around him. Even if he gets angry or sad, he forgets it instantly. His heart is light and free. He finds joy in small things. As a result, his enthusiasm is inexhaustible. He has an insatiable curiosity about everything. These are the hallmarks of a child-like heart.

Some children tell Amma, "My friend's mother is suffering from cancer. His father has no job, and they have no food to eat at home. O Amma, please help his father get a good job!"

All of us have within us such a child-like heart, which longs to share the sorrows of others and to console them. This is manifest in childhood.

A little girl's friend died. The girl went to her friend's home. When she returned, her father asked her, "What did you do there?"

"I consoled my friend's mother," she said.

"How did you do that?" her father asked.

"I sat in her lap and cried with her."

The hearts of children become emotionally attached to other people, birds, animals, flowers and butterflies. They become sad when they see the pain of even a tiny insect. We, too, had this quality when we were children but lost it as we grew older. We have since become embodiments of selfishness and egoism.

There is still a child-like heart within us all. If we can awaken it, we can progress towards a joyful and successful future.

24. Value of Time

Children, we live in a frenetic age. We barely have time to catch our breath as we rush from one task to another.

"Don't just sit idle. Do something!" Since childhood, we have heard our parents and teachers say this. But the time has now come for us to think, "Why not sit still for a while instead of doing something?"

Excessive speed in anything kills its beauty. It is like forcibly opening the petals of a rosebud; we will only rob it of its fragrance and beauty.

Most of the things we pursue will not give us happiness. Not only that, they will take away whatever happiness we had. Some people come with their families to the beach to watch the sunset, but spend their time chatting on their mobile phones instead. Hence, they are not able to appreciate the beauty of the ocean or the glory of the sunset.

Even at home, many people spend their time on Facebook, and neglect to look at the faces of their wife or children sitting right beside them. The wife might be sad over something or the children might be feeling troubled, but the husband or father will not have the time even to look at their faces.

Once, when a man returned home from work, he saw his five-year-old son waiting for him. The boy asked, "Dad, how much do you earn for one hour's work?"

The man replied, "Three hundred rupees."

"Dad, please give me ₹200!"

Thinking that his son wanted the money for a new toy, the father became irritated. "I don't have time for your childish nonsense. Don't speak another word to me!"

The son silently went inside his room and closed the door.

After a while, the father felt that he ought to have been more loving and patient with his son. He opened the door to his son's room and asked, "Son, have you slept?"

"No, dad, I haven't."

"Hope you're not feeling sad because I became angry with you earlier. Here's the ₹200 you asked for. Son, why do you need this money?

The boy's face lit up with joy. He took out a hundred-rupee note from under his pillow. Holding out ₹300 to his father, he said, "Dad, here's ₹300. Will you please spend an hour with me?"

In the midst of your busy life, do not forget to look at the world around you. Share some love, kindness and joy with your family, friends and colleagues. Live in the present moment. Enjoy life.

25. Fruits of Past Deeds

Children, some people ask if God is partial towards some. In this world, some people enjoy good health whereas others are always dogged by illness; some are poor whereas others are rich; some are good-looking, and others, ugly. We cannot blame God for this inequality. We alone are to blame for this. Pure actions reap perfect results. The sorrow of *prārabdha* (consequences of past actions) that we experience today is the result of careless actions in the past. There is no point in blaming God for this. For example, by using genetically modified seeds and chemical fertilizers, we can increase the harvest tenfold. However, doing so will reduce the nutritional value of grains and vegetables drastically. Not only that, as a result of eating such produce, our body becomes contaminated by harmful chemicals. The health of both those who eat such food and their children is impaired. This situation is the result of our selfishness. We cannot blame God for it.

Once, a boss asked his workers to break stones. One worker was physically strong whereas the other was weak. A few days later, the boss went to check on how the work was progressing. He pointed out a large rock each to his workers and asked them to break it. The stronger man struck his rock ten times but was unable to break it, whereas when the weaker man struck his rock just twice, it split open. The stronger man asked the weaker one, "How did you split the rock open after striking it just twice?"

The weaker man replied, "I had already struck it many times with my hammer earlier."

Similarly, if life is easy for some and hard for others, it is because of the actions they performed in the past. Our growth today is the result of good actions performed yesterday. If we want to have a bright future, we must do good deeds in the present. If we do not, we will suffer tomorrow.

That said, when we see someone suffering, we must not think that it is the consequence of his past actions. Instead, we must consider it our duty to help him. If we help those in distress today, we will be spared of suffering tomorrow. By pulling out someone who has fallen into a ditch, we can prevent our own fall in the future.

In a sense, the sorrows arising from prārabdha are a blessing from God as they help us remember him. We can see how those who have never even once called out to God turn to him when they begin to suffer and how they take to the path of righteous living. They can thus find release from the suffering caused by past actions.

26. Learn to Give

Children, until recently, sacrifice and simplicity were regarded as ideals of life. That vision of life has changed. Today, the goals of most people are to make as much money as possible and to enjoy material pleasures. For many, success in life is taking as much as possible from society while giving as little as they can.

In reality, there ought to be a harmonious balance between the individual and society. If we take anything from society or nature, we are obliged to give something back in return. If each person strives to give more than he or she takes, peace, unity and prosperity will prevail in society.

Whether towards our family or society, our attitude towards everyone and everything has become business-minded. Even our relationship with God has become like this. Our attitude towards God and the Guru ought to be one of total surrender. Instead, we calculate even in their presence, wondering how we can gain from them.

Amma remembers a story. Once, a rich businessman went on a cruise. Suddenly, there was a terrible storm. The captain of the ship announced that their chances of survival were slim. Everyone on board started praying. The businessman prayed, "O Lord, if I survive, I shall sell my five-star hotel and donate 75% of the money to You. Please save me!"

Miraculously, the sea became calm at once and everyone reached the destination safely. The businessman was disturbed. He thought "Oh dear, if I sell the hotel, I can earn at least 1 *crore*

(10 million) rupees. I have pledged 75% of the sales to the Lord. Do I really need to give him so much? What to do?" He started pondering on ways to get out of this quandary.

The next day, an advertisement appeared in the newspaper: "Five-star hotel for sale. Price: One rupee only!"

There was a huge demand to buy the hotel. The businessman announced, "I am selling this hotel for a rupee. However, there is one condition: the person who wishes to purchase the hotel must also buy my dog, which is priced at 10 million rupees."

Eventually, the hotel was sold. The businessman then went to the temple and offered 75 *paisa* to the Lord.

Such is the attitude many people have. They are ready to cheat even God to gain their own ends.

We see the world today with the eyes of a businessman. No matter what the sphere, we seek only our own advancement. We might make progress with such an attitude, but such progress is dangerous. Cancer cells grow unchecked and, as a result, cause the individual's death. Similarly, 'progress' that is detrimental to society is never true progress. Eventually, it will cause the destruction of both the individual and society. Everyone has the right to grow and expand. However, our growth should also help others grow.

In truth, whatever we give the world comes back to us. If we sow a seed, the earth returns a harvest that is a hundred-fold more than what we sowed. The merit accruing from good actions helps us not only in our present life but also ensures an auspicious future. The real success of life lies in giving more than taking.

27. I am Love. Love is my very Nature

Children, what people yearn for most in this world is love. People make friends, get married and start families only for love. Yet, the greatest poverty in the world today is the lack of love. Everyone wants to receive love but no one wants to give it. If we love, we do so with many strings attached in the form of expectations and conditions. Such relationships can fall apart at any moment. Such love can become hatred and enmity. This is the nature of the world. If we understand this, we will not suffer. The nature of fire is heat and light. Expecting fire to have only light and not heat is unrealistic. Likewise, if we can accept that worldly love inevitably brings sorrow, we will be able to face each and every situation with equanimity.

There is pure love in everyone. All of us have the capacity to love others without expectation. As love is our very nature, we can never lose it. A diamond left lying inside a bottle of oil may seem lusterless. But if we wipe away the thick coating of oil, we can restore brilliance to the diamond. Similarly, if we eliminate the impurities of the mind, we can regain the most pristine form of love.

The ladder of love has many rungs. At present, many of us are at the lowest rung. We must not spend the rest of our life there. We must slowly climb up the ladder, rung by rung. We can thus reach the highest rung of love and fulfil our lives.

People usually say, "I love you." But the truth is that "I am love. Love is my very nature." When we say "I love you," there are two entities: 'I' and 'you.' There is a gap between the two. Love is crushed in this gap.

From this perspective of 'I' and 'you,' loving another with expectation is like a tiny rat snake attempting to swallow a huge frog, a tortuous ordeal for both. Conversely, if we love without any expectation, we will never feel sorrow. Our selfless love will awaken selfless love in others. Life then becomes filled with love and joy. We realize that "love is my very nature." Thereafter, we become free of desire and expectation. Our love will be like a river, a free flow that touches and purifies one and all. Everything we do will be of benefit to the world. May all of us be able to rise to the level of such pure love.

28. Efficient Action

Children, stress is now a common problem that affects even small children. When a machine becomes overheated, it will malfunction. In the same way, tension adversely affects our mental capabilities and efficiency. It is natural to become stressed in unfavorable circumstances or when faced with danger. But if we are always stressed, it will impair our very functionality. Frequent stress not only affects our ability to act, it also causes all kinds of diseases. Instead, if the mind is calm and peaceful, we will be able to think clearly and assess situations properly.

Once, a farmer lost his watch in a haystack. He was very fond of his watch, which his grandfather had given him as a birthday present when he was a child. He rummaged through the haystack for a long time. Failing to find his watch, he became disheartened and stopped searching. There were children playing football nearby. Approaching them, he asked them if they would help him find his watch. The children combed through the haystack but failed to find the watch. When the farmer had almost given up hope of finding the watch, one of the children came up to him and asked for another chance to find the watch. The farmer agreed. The boy went into the barn where the hay was stored. A few minutes later, he came out with the missing watch.

The farmer was astonished. When he asked the boy the secret of his success, the boy said, "For some time, I just sat still on the floor and listened carefully. In the silence, I heard the ticking sound of the watch coming from one corner of the haystack. Then it was easy to find the watch."

This story clearly shows how a calm mind can think clearly and find solutions to problems easily.

There are many ways to relieve tension. We can enjoy the beauty of nature, appreciate music, and take part in games and activities that relax the mind. Spending time with friends and small children can also help to reduce tension. Slow and regulated breathing, yōga postures like the *śavāsana* (corpse pose), and meditation are especially beneficial in alleviating tension and becoming relaxed.

But more important than all these is adopting a healthy approach to life. We must cultivate an awareness that will help us maintain an inner balance at all times instead of soaring in victory or sinking in failure. If we do so, our mind will become calm and peaceful, and we can become more efficient in action.

29. Try Not to Repeat Your Mistakes

Children, rare are those who have not made mistakes knowingly or unknowingly in life. Most people brood over the mistakes they made and feel bad about it. It is futile to continue feeling troubled over past actions. What is over is over. If we continue brooding over them, we will lose whatever reserves of strength we have left. Instead, we must strongly resolve, "I will not repeat my mistakes again!" The pure efforts we put forth afterwards will cleanse the mind. This is what is needed. The mind's purity is revealed by the desire to think noble thoughts and do good deeds, and by the efforts made in that direction.

There is no sin that cannot be washed away by the tears of remorse. However, once we know what is wrong, we must not do it again. The mind must gird itself to walk the right path. If a young child throws a toy at his mother, she will smile lovingly, gather him into her arms and kiss him. But if he does the same thing after he has grown up, she will not tolerate it. Similarly, God will forgive the sins we committed unknowingly, but He will not forgive the sins we commit after we have understood what is right and wrong. Therefore, we must try not to repeat our mistakes.

If we make a mistake while writing with a pencil, we can erase it. But we can only do so once or twice. If we keep erasing, the paper will tear. The greatest sin is knowingly repeating the same mistake. We must avoid this at all costs.

Do not think, "I have sinned many times. My mind isn't pure enough to pray. I'll start praying after my mind has been purified." We will never be able to swim in the ocean if we wait for its waves to subside. Can you imagine a doctor telling a patient to consult him only after he has been healed? We go to a doctor to cure our illness. Similarly, God must cleanse our hearts. Only by taking refuge in him can the mind be purified.

We need not remain sad, thinking about the kind of life we used to lead. The past is like a cancelled check. We need not continue lamenting over our past mistakes and failures. We still have with us invaluable capital—life. Hence, we must think about the great profits we stand to gain. Optimism lends vitality to life, even amidst the greatest sorrows. We must never lose our optimistic faith. God's grace will certainly protect us.

30. Sharing

Children, people face two kinds of the poverty: first, the poverty caused by a lack of money, depriving one of even necessities like food, clothing and shelter; second, the poverty caused by the depletion of love and compassion in society. Of these, the second kind of poverty deserves more attention because it is the basis of the first kind of poverty. If we have mutual love and compassion, we will be able to ease the troubles of those suffering from financial poverty. However, people today are retreating within themselves, whether in villages or towns. The culture of sharing is disappearing, even among spouses. Society can maintain its balance only if we focus more on giving than taking. But today, most only want to take.

There was a man who only wanted to take from others. He never shared anything with anyone. He dedicated his life to amassing more and more wealth. One day, while walking somewhere, he tripped and fell into a deep pit by the roadside. He tried hard to get out but failed. Helplessly, he started shouting "Help... help..." After some time, a passer-by heard his shouts and came to the pit. He held his hand out to the man and said, "Give me your hand!" But the man in the pit did not. Even after the passer-by repeatedly asked, "Give me your hand," the man refused to raise his hand. Finally, the passer-by stretched out his hand again and said, "Take hold of my hand!" As soon as he heard this, the man in the pit reached out to grab the passer-by's hand and was thus rescued.

Many of us are like the man who fell into the pit. We know only how to take from others. Such selfishness can only lead to the decline of society.

We must cultivate a mind that yearns to give rather than take. Our survival hinges on mutual dependence. Our lives should not be for ourselves alone. We are here in this world for a short time only. Just like the butterfly, which gives joy and cheerfulness to others in its short lifespan of a few days, every second of our life should benefit others. We must share our wealth and joy with others. Through mutual dependence, love and sharing, we must become one.

31. Giving and Taking

Children, the biggest obstacles standing in the way of our enjoying bliss in life are the sense of 'I' and our selfish thoughts. We are unable to forget ourselves and love others. Our attitude at present can be expressed thus: "I want everything. I want to make everything my own." Without changing this attitude, we cannot experience joy in life. Therefore, instead of thinking about what we can get from others, let us foster the desire to give. The one who loves to give is like a king whereas the one who wishes only to take is like a beggar.

Amma remembers a story. Once, a man went to visit his friend, whom he had not seen in years. While standing on the lawn and taking in the beauty of the mansion his friend was staying in, the friend came out. After exchanging pleasantries, the visitor asked, "Your house is beautiful! Who else lives here apart from you?"

"I'm staying here alone."

"All alone? Is this your house?"

"Yes."

"How did you make enough money to buy such a big house at this young age?"

"My older brother is a millionaire. He built this house for me."

Observing his friend's silence, the host said, "I can guess what you're thinking. You were wishing that you, too, had a millionaire brother, weren't you?"

The man replied, "No, I was thinking that if I were a millionaire, like your brother, I would also have built such a mansion for my younger brother."

Children, such is the attitude we should have. Learn to give. Only one who gives has the right to take. One who is generous will be welcome everywhere. What we have taken and experienced will be lost in a moment, but what we have given and shared will remain with us forever—as contentment, peace and prosperity.

When we lose the impulse to give, we pave the way for the downfall of society. Even if we cannot nurture children who long only to give, we should at least try to inculcate in them the desire to give as well as to take. Only then can harmony prevail in the country and the world.

Children, we may lack the wherewithal to help others financially, but we can at least smile at them sincerely or speak pleasantly to them, can't we? What does it cost us? One who does not feel compassion for others cannot be considered a devotee. Compassion is the first step of spirituality. Compassionate people need not go anywhere in search of God. He will rush to where the compassionate are, for the kind heart is his favorite abode.

32. Do Good

Children, we live in a world that is filled with selfishness. Most people are concerned only with taking as much as they can from others. What the world needs now are people who are more concerned with giving than taking. If a few people who are prepared to spread the message of selflessness through the example of their own lives come forward, we can turn earth into heaven.

Once, a Guru was telling the disciples in his āśram about the variety in human nature. He filled four glasses with water. He dropped a stone into the first glass. There was no change in the water. The stone sank to the bottom of the glass. He then dropped a clod of mud into the second glass. The mud dissolved in the water, making it murky. He dropped a wad of cotton into the third glass. The cotton slowly soaked up all the water and became bloated. He put a piece of rock candy into the fourth glass. The candy dissolved in the water, making it sweet.

Pointing to the four glasses, the Guru said, "They represent four types of people. Most people can be compared to a stone. They will neither improve nor will their lives benefit others.

"The second type is like the clod of mud. Not only will they do no good to society, they will also pollute the minds of those who come into contact with them. They pollute the minds of everyone in society.

"The third type is like the wad of cotton that has been dropped into water. They are totally selfish. They will strive to grab everything in the world for themselves and for their own enjoyment. They will hoard wealth but will never help others at all.

"The fourth type is like rock candy. They spread sweetness in the lives of others. Such people ought to be our role models. If we follow their example, our lives will also be filled with sweetness. Slowly, our sweetness will infuse the lives of others."

You may wonder how one person can make a difference to the world. Even small acts of goodness touch many people. For example, when we smile, others smile in return. Likewise, the good deeds that we do will inspire others to do good.

Let us not waste any opportunity to do even an insignificant act of goodness. Just as countless drops of water become a river, the small acts of goodness that we do today will be instrumental in bringing about a major social transformation tomorrow.

33. Giving

Children, we can never get enough of wealth. Nevertheless, we can make the best use of it by donating to people who are struggling in life and who need money badly.

When going on pilgrimages, we carry money with us to give as alms to beggars. We set aside coins for this purpose and will be careful not to give anyone more than five rupees. The aim of giving is to lessen our selfishness. But we are miserly even in giving. However rich we may be, our wealth will not remain with us forever. We must help the suffering as much as we can. Real wealth is that which helps others.

Before giving, we must first know whom we are giving to and what they need. We may give food and clothing, but not money, to unfamiliar beggars. If we give them money, they might use it for drink or drugs. Thus, by giving them money, we are giving them an opportunity to do wrong.

We must give generously to those who lack the means to work, to orphans, to the destitute elderly, and to the ailing who have no money to buy medicine. It is our *dharma*, our duty, to do so. But we must be careful that our aim is not name and fame.

The residents of a nursing home and guests were enjoying the cultural programs being presented as part of the nursing home's anniversary. Suddenly, a man entered the hall where the function was taking place and switched off all the fans. He was a prominent businessman from that city. One of the residents asked him, "Why did you switch off the fans? The heat is unbearable."

The merchant said, "I was the one who donated all the fans in this nursing home. My name is printed on them. But if the fans are whirling all the time, no one will see my name. I switched off the fans so that those attending today's function know that I donated the fans."

Such donation cannot be called giving at all. The businessman's attitude might even cause him to lose the spiritual merit he earned through his donation.

The attitude of the person who gives is of utmost importance. When a wealthy man donates for the sake of gaining fame or with some other selfish motive in mind, his donation is degraded into a mere commercial transaction. But when one gives, seeing God in others, at personal cost and without expecting anything in return, the results of that giving will be truly great.

34. Head and Heart

Children, spiritual teachers often give more importance to the heart than to the head. Of course, intelligence is necessary; Amma will never say otherwise. In truth, the head and heart are not two. If we have a discerning intellect, our mind will naturally become expansive. From expansiveness arises innocence, the readiness to compromise, humility and an attitude of mutual co-operation. The heart is a synonym for expansiveness.

However, today, our intelligence is often impaired. Selfishness and arrogance govern our thinking, and this is the cause of all sorrow in life. When arrogance increases, we become more narrow-minded and less willing to compromise. An expansive and accommodating mind is necessary in both worldly and spiritual life.

Suppose a man lays down certain laws at home: his wife should live, speak and behave in certain ways only because she is his wife. If he insists that she follows these rules, will there be peace at home? No! Suppose he does not utter even a single word to his wife and children after returning home from work. If he continues to behave like an executive at home, going to his room and looking over his papers, will his family members appreciate it? If he justifies himself by saying that this is how he is, will they be able to accept it? No. Conversely, if he speaks pleasantly to his wife and spends some time with his children, everyone will be happy. There will be peace at home. It is this attitude that is being referred to when we talk about the heart.

Today, our most dominant characteristic is selfishness, and it has edged discernment out. This absence is making itself felt in life. It is difficult for society to enjoy peace and progress without a give-and-take attitude. Just as a machine needs to be greased regularly to prevent it from rusting, we must be humble and ready to compromise in order to facilitate the journey of life. There are times when we must use our intelligence, but we must use it discerningly. Similarly, we must give the heart due importance whenever the situation warrants it.

When we give due importance to the heart, humility and an attitude of co-operation will grow in us. Peace and contentment will blossom. The goal of spirituality is also broad-mindedness, for only one with an expansive mind can realize God. The Self is beyond the reach of logic and intelligence; it is a subjective experience. If we wish to savor the sweetness of the Self, we must cultivate the qualities of the heart more than the those of the head.

35. Revenge

Children, disaster unexpectedly strikes the lives of many of us. The sudden death of a loved one or unbearable financial losses can make us lose our mental balance. We may then feel overwhelmed by sorrow and disappointment. If anyone is responsible for this pain, we might feel intense anger towards that person. That anger can lead to a strong desire to take revenge. However, if we are careful not to act indiscriminately, we can lead the mind back to the right path. To do so, we must calm the mind at once. Only a calm mind can think clearly. Strong and uncontrolled emotions affect one's discernment and impair one's memory. Hence, instead of reacting impulsively, we must calm the mind down first so that we can think clearly and ascertain the causes for the disaster that befell us.

Amma remembers a story. A drunken driver knocked into a young man, killing him. The young man's mother could not bear the sorrow of her son's untimely death. For days on end, she remained lost in memories of her beloved son. She was overwhelmed by grief, which slowly transformed into the desire for revenge. She decided to kill the driver to avenge her son's death. But when her mind became calmer, another thought entered her mind: "If I kill him, will my son come back to life? No. Not only that, I suffered unbearable anguish because of my son's death. If I kill that man, his mother and loved ones will suffer so much. Why must they grieve because of me? No one else should suffer the misfortune I did." She reflected further. "The car knocked my son down because the driver was drunk. If he wasn't drunk, this wouldn't have happened. So, the real cause of this tragedy is alcohol. If I launch a campaign to increase awareness among people of the dangers of drinking and driving, such accidents can be reduced."

She enlisted the help of some friends to increase awareness among people about the perils of alcoholism; she spent the rest of her life in this way. Her earnest efforts led to the creation of a large organization dedicated to helping addicts recover.

If she had killed the man who killed her son, how much harm would have befallen her! Not just that, the world would not have benefited in any way from the act of revenge. Once she realized the real cause of her son's death, she was able to harness her anger to serve a noble purpose. This benefitted both her and society.

We usually do not try to find out the real cause of our problems. This is why they never cease. If we calmly seek their real causes, like the mother in this story did, we can channel our anger and desire for revenge along an outlet that benefits society. If we strive to find out calmly the reasons for our problems instead of reacting impulsively, we will be able to do a lot of good in the world.

36. Anger and Revenge

Children, all around us, we hear stories of anger and revenge. We can see this everywhere in society—in poems, stories and novels. Most movies and TV serials revolve around these themes. Amma feels that this theme has now spread to cartoons even! Even when cartoon characters fight against evil, their actions are often violent and cruel. As a result, the idea that violence and cruelty are acceptable ways of countering evil grows in the minds of even small children. Amma does not like this trend.

We must probe into the primary cause of hatred and anger. We feel anger towards someone when he does not behave according to our expectations. When we expect love from someone but do not receive it, we feel anger towards him. Conversely, we feel happy when someone respects us or smiles at us. By the same logic, everyone wants to be loved and respected by others. Understanding this, we must be ready to love and respect everyone.

Seeing her young child crying loudly, the mother gave her a toy, which distracted the child for some time. A short while later, the child started crying loudly again. If the mother gives her another toy, the child might stop crying for a short time. But she was not crying for toys in the first place: she was hungry and crying for milk. The child's tears and anguish will end only when the mother finds out the reason for her tears and feeds her. Similarly, we must find within ourselves the causes of our anger and hatred instead of searching for temporary peace and joy.

Amma remembers the story of a devotee who went on a pilgrimage to end his pain and sorrow. He traveled for many days and endured a lot of hardship to reach a holy place. It was crowded with devotees. While everyone was praying silently before the sacred shrine, someone accidentally stepped on his foot. Unable to control his anger, the man forgot his surroundings and shouted furiously at the devotee who had accidentally stepped on him. He not only lost his own peace of mind, he also shattered the peace and tranquility pervading that hallowed site by rudely interrupting the one-pointed prayers of so many people. Children, never behave like this. The purpose of *japa* (repeated chanting of the mantra), prayer and pilgrimages is to gain noble qualities such as patience and equipoise. Only when we have these qualities can we experience real peace and joy.

Their own hatred and vengefulness caused Rāvaṇa and Duryōdhana to destroy not only themselves but also their clan and country. Never forget that those who harbor grudges destroy not only others but themselves as well. May goodness shine in my children.

37. Temper

Children, one of the key reasons for the breakup of relationships is reckless anger. We often get angry over trivial matters. If we exercise a little self-control, we can avoid many problems caused by anger. Sometimes, because of a misunderstanding, we lose our temper even with innocent people. No matter how many times we beg their forgiveness after realizing our mistake, their wounded hearts will never forgive us completely. Therefore, we must learn to control our temper. If something makes us angry, we must exercise patience instead of reacting impulsively. Gradually, we will be able to conquer the habit of losing our temper.

A woman told her friend, "Every day, when my husband comes home from work, we start fighting. Is there any way to avoid this?"

The friend said, "Don't worry. I have just the right medicine with me. As soon as your husband starts speaking angrily, take a mouthful of this medicine. Don't swallow it. Just keep it inside your mouth." Saying so, the friend gave her the bottle of medicine.

That evening, as soon as her husband became angry, the woman poured the medicine into her mouth. After some time, the husband cooled down. The same thing happened for the next two days also. The wife was amazed. The next day, she told her friend, "Your medicine is really effective! We haven't fought for three days. Please tell me how to prepare this medicine so that I can make it myself."

Her friend said, "I'll tell you, but let's wait for another six months."

Six months passed. There were no more fights in the house, which was now filled with love and peace. One day, the friend said, "I shall now share the secret of the medicine. It has no special ingredients. Actually, it's just plain water. When you held it in your mouth and could not speak, your husband's mind became calm. Your mind also gained some time to calm down. That's all."

This story makes it clear that if we are ready to forbear a little, life will become peaceful and happy.

When we are angry, we should refrain from speaking the words that come to mind. We should also desist from acting upon the decisions we make then. Anger is like an open wound in the mind. We must first try to heal the wound.

Patience and discernment are the only antidotes to anger. When we reflect on matters, we will gain the ability to perceive our own weaknesses. We will see our thoughts reflected clearly, as if in a clean mirror. We will understand the pettiness of anger and realize the greatness of forgiving.

38. War and Conflict

Children, many great souls have worked tirelessly for world peace, and many are still striving today. Yet, we do not see much change in the world. War, conflict, poverty and starvation exist even today. Many ask if there is a lasting solution to these problems.

The war and conflict that we see in the world today are outer expressions of the inner conflicts raging in human minds. The mind ought to become our obedient servant, but at present, it is lording over and manipulating us. The hatred, anger and cruelty in human minds are far more lethal than all the explosives in the outer world. If we do not flush out these toxic emotions, war and conflict will continue to prevail in the world.

Once, a nightingale was perched on a tree and singing sweetly. A hunter trapped the bird and wanted to kill it. The bird gazed piteously into the hunter's eyes and begged, "Please don't kill me. Let me go!" The nightingale's heart-breaking plea moved the hunter. In that moment, he became aware of the stark difference between the nightingale, darting about blissfully and warbling sweetly, and his own heinous and cruel life. He told the nightingale, "I shall release you on one condition: you must tell me the secret of your joy."

The nightingale said, "I'm scared of you. First, let me go, and then I shall tell you the secret of my joy."

The hunter released the bird. As the nightingale flew away, she said, "It is the evil in you that causes you such pain and misery. Your heart is completely darkened by cruelty whereas we never hurt anyone. The goodness in our hearts is the reason for our joy."

The nightingale's words opened the eyes of the hunter. He forsook the path of cruelty and embarked on a new path in life.

Our hearts ought to melt in compassion when we see the pain and misery of others. The compassion in our hearts must be reflected in our actions. Compassion is the one-word answer to all problems in the world. If we have to provide an answer in two words, they would be love and compassion. The answer in three words would be love, compassion and patience. War and conflict will end only when individual minds become filled with compassion.

39. Criticism

Children, it is natural to feel sorrow, anger and despair when criticized. But such responses drain us of our energy. However, if we do not allow emotions to enslave us and instead kindle our discernment, we will be able to face criticism with equanimity and learn from criticisms. We can thus make progress and succeed in life.

It is not easy to become aware of our own mistakes and weaknesses. Therefore, we ought to see our critics as our best teachers, because they help us realize our shortcomings. Those who praise us will not be able to do that. But when others criticize us or express their dislike for us, we must do some soul searching: "Why did they criticize me? Did I do anything wrong to elicit that criticism?" In this way, we can turn criticisms and accusations into stepping stones for our growth.

A child will become embarrassed and upset if friends point out stains in his clothes. He may even feel resentment towards them. But if someone tells a grownup about the stains on her clothes, she will not feel even the slightest resentment against that person, only gratitude. She will not feel embarrassed either because she will not see the stains as a personal shortcoming. But the child does not have such discernment. Hence, such situations will distress him and make him upset.

However, if a grownup's behavior or actions are criticized, she will naturally feel upset and react in anger. She will not demonstrate the same detachment she did when the stains on her clothes were pointed out to her, because she identifies with her own behavior and actions. She is unable to view them dispassionately, like a witness. If she can do so, she will be able to accept any criticism or accusation calmly, and correct herself if it is valid. If she goes one step further, she will even thank those who criticized her. Should the criticisms and accusations be unfounded, she will laugh them off.

Just as a lotus stem draws all the nourishment it needs from the mud it is rooted in, and brings forth beautiful and fragrant lotus flowers, we must learn to gain awareness and energy from the mire of criticism. If we can do so, the vine of our lives will yield the blossoms of peace and happiness.

40. Spirituality and Poverty

Children, some people say that the reason for poverty in Bhārat (India) is her spiritual culture. But spirituality is not an obstacle to earning wealth or making material progress. On the contrary, spirituality fosters even material progress. Earning wealth has long been accepted as one of the goals of life, together with *dharma* (righteous living) and *mōkṣa* (spiritual liberation). However, we must be careful not to accumulate wealth unethically or for selfish reasons.

Long ago, the people of India were steeped in spirituality. For this very reason, she was also materially prosperous. But gradually, some people started becoming greedier. They began to compete with each other for wealth, power and position. Their pride and jealousy made them abandon dharma and forget God. Discord intensified, adversely affecting the country's unity and strength, and this, in turn, led to conquest by colonial powers, who ruled India for many centuries. They plundered the country of its wealth and left it utterly bereft of riches. How hard it would be to sow a seed in a desert and nurture it until it sprouts and becomes a healthy sapling! Such is the state of this country; we must work hard to make it lush and green again.

Sadly, the truth is that we have not learnt even from such bitter experiences. The majority are focused on personal gain rather than national development. They do not realize that true material prosperity can be gained only by embracing spirituality.

If we continue like this, forgetting our own heritage, we will suffer greatly for it.

Nature has provided enough for the country's sustainable development. If we utilize our resources properly, there will be no poverty here. But after India became independent, we did not harness our natural resources properly. Whereas other countries are turning deserts into farmlands, we are turning our fertile fields into wastelands. Rural development is still not a priority. For this to happen, educated youth must go the villages and make the villagers aware of the government schemes supporting them. They should motivate people to regard the country as their own home. They must inspire people to use farmlands for agricultural activities. At the same time, they must also share our spiritual culture with them.

Spirituality teaches us to give more than we take from society. When we assimilate spiritual principles, we become more considerate towards others. We will begin to see others as ourselves and be willing to share whatever resources we have with them. The ancient sages advised us to make money with a hundred hands and to share it with a thousand hands. If we assimilate this message, India's future will be glorious.

41. Transformation

Children, there is no one who does not long for change. Everyone wants to overcome his or her physical and mental weaknesses and to be free from negative emotions and habits. But most of us do not have a clear idea about how to change.

It is difficult to change one's nature. Hence, we often change only our behavior, not our character. Instead of eliminating the ego, many of us artfully conceal it and wear the mask of humility. We suppress or hide emotions such as anger, jealousy and hatred. However, by suppressing an emotion, we can neither keep it at bay nor prevent it from arising again.

Once, some miscreants scattered sharp thorns in the front yards of two next-door neighbors. When he saw the thorns in the morning, one of the neighbors covered the thorns with a layer of earth and thus dealt with the problem. The second neighbor patiently picked up each one of the thorns, threw them into a bonfire and reduced them to ash. Both of them solved the problem. But what will happen when it rains? The first man's front yard will be full of thorns. Not only that, he will have to work twice as hard as the second man did to remove all the thorns. Such is the case with negative emotions, too. Even if we succeed in suppressing them temporarily, it does not mean that we have eradicated them permanently.

Instead of suppressing or concealing negative tendencies, we must confront them with the weapons of alertness and discernment. First of all, we must firmly resolve never again to become enslaved by such emotions and thoughts. Every time such thoughts arise, we must notice them and withdraw the mind from them. Then, we must find out why such thoughts arise and strive to eliminate the causes.

The main reason we act upon our *vāsanās* (latent tendencies) is our lack of alertness. If the watchman guarding the house at night remains awake and alert, and carries his lantern while patrolling the grounds, no thief will be able to break into the house. A person who firmly resolves never to give in to any weakness and who observes each and every thought arising in the mind will notice every negative thought that arises in his alert mind and thus control it.

No bad habit can be eliminated at once. However, constant effort and a strong determination will lead us to victory. We can thus transform our lives completely.

42. Meditation

Children, real knowledge is learning how to focus the mind. This is possible through meditation.

Meditation helps to reduce stress and relieve anxiety. Through meditation, we can enjoy bliss and peace of mind. Meditation enhances our beauty, life span, strength, health, intelligence and energy.

We must first learn how to meditate properly in solitude. It is not necessary that one has to believe in God in order to meditate. There are many meditation techniques. During meditation, we can focus the mind on any part of the body or concentrate on a point, or we can imagine becoming one with the infinite. If we like gazing at the flame of a lamp, we can do so. We can light a candle or lamp in a dark room and gaze at the flame for a long time. The flame should not flicker. We can also visualize that flame in the heart or between the eyebrows. We can focus on the inner effulgence that arises as we look at the lamp. Those who like meditating on a form can imagine their *iṣṭa-dēvatā* (preferred form of divinity) standing in the middle of the flame. But it is better to visualize the iṣṭa-dēvatā standing amidst the flames of a sacrificial fire, for we can then imagine offering our jealousy, ego and other negativities into the blazing sacrificial fire.

For beginners, meditation on a form is easier than meditation on the formless. Meditating on the iṣṭa-dēvatā helps the mind become focused on him or her. The *sattvic* qualities[8] of the iṣṭa-dēvatā will also grow in us. Place a small picture of your favorite deity in front of you. Sit and gaze at the picture for some time. Then, close your eyes and try to visualize that form clearly in your mind. When the clarity of the form fades, open your eyes and gaze at the picture again. Then, close your eyes once again and imagine that you are talking to your iṣṭa-dēvatā. Mentally embrace the iṣṭa-dēvatā and plead, "O Lord, please do not leave me!" If we constantly meditate like this with attentiveness, the iṣṭa-dēvatā's form will dawn clearly in the heart.

It is the nature of the mind to wander. Therefore, meditation is like trying to push hollow driftwood into water; when we let go, it will drift up to the surface at once. Such is the mind. Hence, in the initial stages of meditation, we might need to apply some pressure on the mind to make it meditate. But once we acquire a taste for meditation, we need not force the mind anymore. Meditation will become joyful.

If we practice meditation regularly, the mind will gradually become calmer until it becomes crystal clear. The Supreme Self will shine in the calm mind, like the reflection of the sun in a still lake.

---

[8] *Sattva* is one of the three *guṇas* (attributes or modes of existence), which includes *rajas* and *tamas*. *Sattva* is associated with harmony, goodness, truth and serenity.

43. Conceptions of Divinity

Children, some people criticize as primitive the worship of Gaṇapati, who has the head of an elephant, and Hanumān, who has the body of a monkey. At first glance, such a criticism might seem valid. However, if we study this subject in greater depth, we will come to realize the lofty principles, ideals and goals behind the worship of such forms.

Amma has seen paintings on the walls of many homes in the West. Once, Amma saw a painting that an ordinary person would not understand: a few brush strokes in just four or five colors. It looked as if someone had dipped a broom in paint and smeared the canvas with it! But this painting was worth $500,000. Guards had been hired to protect it, and security cameras had been installed. Although we did not understand the painting, the owners were able to talk about it for hours on end. No one considers the painter a fool. On the contrary, he is hailed as a great artist. No one asks the owners of the painting why they paid such an exorbitant price for the painting when so many people are starving. The value of the painting is not diminished just because ordinary people cannot understand its meaning. Similarly, only when we can understand the principles behind the deities in the Hindu religion will we appreciate their greatness.

Bhārat's (India's) real wealth is her culture. But we do not strive to understand it. Our faith is confined to traditional rituals and festivals. But this faith is so flimsy that, when someone criticizes it just a little, we lose it. Therefore, we must put forth some effort to understand the scientific basis of our culture.

In Sanātana Dharma, God is the all-pervading consciousness beyond attributes, names and forms. However, He can assume any form to bless devotees. Just as the wind can waft as a gentle breeze, blow as a strong gust, or even beat heavily as a hurricane, the Almighty Lord, who controls the wind, can adopt unlimited *bhāvas* (divine moods). Hence, we worship the one God in diverse forms such as Viṣṇu, Śiva, Gaṇapati, Hanumān, Durgā and Saraswatī.

God's diverse qualities are illumined in the various deities. Hanumān represents the principle of subduing the restless monkey mind. The *praṇava* ('Ōm') is the primal sound. Therefore, Gaṇapati, who is of the form of the praṇava, deserves to be worshipped first. Similarly, there are subtle meanings in the forms of all the deities. No matter which form of divinity we worship, finally, we will attain the formless Supreme Truth.

44. Practice of Japa

Children, how to control the mind and make it focused: this is a problem that haunts most people. All we need to do is close our eyes to see how restless the mind is. Even while praying in the temple, our thoughts will be on the chores that need to be completed when we reach home. *Mantra-japa*, the repeated chanting of the mantra, is the process by which the restless mind can be bound to a single thought. By constantly chanting any name or mantra, the bewildering variety of thoughts is reduced and the mind becomes more focused.

"Post no bills"—with just these three words, we can ensure that the wall is not plastered with advertisements or notices. Similarly, with just one thought, i.e. the mantra, we can stop the wanderings of the mind. Reducing thoughts is good for health and increases our lifespan.

One might ask, "Won't thoughts arise even while chanting the mantra?" Even if other thoughts arise then, they will not be too harmful. A thought is like a child. When the child is asleep, the mother can work without any disturbance. But once her child wakes up and starts crying, she will find it difficult to finish her chores. Similarly, the thoughts that arise while we are chanting are not dangerous; they will not trouble us.

It is best to start chanting after the Guru has initiated us into a mantra. In order to make yogurt, we add a little yogurt to milk. Similarly, in order to gain the full benefits of chanting, we must receive a mantra from the Guru. That said, we need not wait until then to practice japa. We can start practicing by chanting a divine name or mantra that we like. For example, we can chant *"Ōm namaḥ śivāya," "Ōm namō nārāyaṇāya," "Ōm parāśaktyai namaḥ"* or any other mantra. Those who like the name of Christ, Allah or the Buddha may chant that name.

While chanting, we can concentrate either on the form of our beloved deity or on the sound of the mantra. With every repetition of the mantra, we can imagine that we are offering a flower at the feet of our beloved deity. Or we can concentrate on each syllable of the mantra. Whichever technique we adopt, what matters is that we do not allow the mind to wander. We must restrict it to remembrance of the Lord.

We can do japa at any time. We can chant while just sitting idly, walking or traveling; these are ideal times to practice japa. It is only when japa becomes habitual that the uncontrolled surge of thoughts will subside. Keep a rosary with you at all times. Use it to maintain a certain count of mantra iterations daily. Doing so will help to foster the habit of chanting.

Initially, we should not chant for long periods of time. Doing so can cause physical and mental problems. At first, do japa for a short period, and then gradually increase the japa until it becomes a habit. Thereafter, the mind will chant continuously without any effort.

Some people chant one mantra for a few days. Then, thinking that it is not potent enough, they start chanting another 'more powerful' mantra. Periodically changing the mantra will not help us. No matter what the mantra is, regular and disciplined chanting will gradually still the mind. Therefore, one must stick to one mantra.

As japa can be easily practiced by anyone, most religions acknowledge it as a *sādhana* (spiritual practice). The disciplined practice of japa bestows peace and concentration on the mind.

It will help us perform our daily activities with greater skill and efficiency.

45. Sacrifice

Children, the goal of human life is everlasting peace and freedom. When this awareness becomes deeply rooted in the mind, the desire for worldly objects will fall away. That said, we cannot call this sacrifice. Sacrifice becomes complete only when we give up the 'I and mine' attitude. More than what we renounce, what matters is the attitude behind the act.

If our own child falls sick, we will take him to the hospital. If we cannot find any vehicle to take us there, we will walk to the hospital with the child, even if the hospital is far away. We will be ready to plead with any number of people in the hospital in order to get our child admitted. If there is no private room available, we will go to the general ward and lie down on the floor with our child. We will take many days off from work to nurse our child back to health. But all these troubles, which are for the sake of our own child, cannot be considered acts of renunciation. We are ready to go to court any number of times to gain a single *cent*[9] of land. We do so for the sake of property ownership. We might forgo sleep to work overtime in order to make more money. We cannot call any of these acts of renunciation. Sacrificing one's own pleasures and comforts to help another person is renunciation. Working hard, enduring hardship, and using the money thus earned to help a poor person is renunciation. When the child from a neighboring house falls sick, and we are ready to stay with her in the hospital without

[9] A cent is 0.01 acres.

expecting anything in return, not even a smile, we can call it renunciation.

Actions done without the attitude of 'I' and 'mine' for the welfare of the world and as an offering to God are the noblest instances of renunciation. Such self-sacrificing acts open the doors to the world of the Self. Only such actions can be called karma-yōga. In contrast, giving up anything with an attitude of 'I' and 'mine' is not worthy of being called a sacrifice.

There was once a rich man who wanted to become a *sanyāsī* (ordained monk). He donated all his wealth to many noble causes benefiting people. Then, he became a sanyāsī, went to a mountain top, built a small hut there, and started staying in it. On learning that there was a sanyāsī living on the mountaintop, many people went to see him. He only had one thing to say to all of them: "Do you know who I am? Do you know how rich I used to be? It is I who donated money for the huge school building that you can see from here. I was also the one who donated money to build the hospital next to the school. The temple that you see was also built with money I donated." Though he had given up all his wealth to take up the life of a monk, he still retained the 'I' sense. How can this be considered renunciation?

When we greet a friend whom we have not seen for a long time, we might present him with a bouquet of flowers. It is we who first enjoy the beauty and the fragrance of the flowers. It is also we who enjoy the satisfaction of giving. Likewise, through selfless service, we gain bliss and contentment even without our knowing. If one who sincerely does selfless service cannot chant his mantra or meditate owing to a lack of time, he need not worry; he will attain immortality. His self-sacrificing life will benefit everyone else. The company of such a person is the greatest *satsaṅg.*

46. Prayer and Faith

Quite a few devotees sorrowfully tell Amma that even after many years of praying, their griefs and misfortunes have not let up. Most people pray either for the fulfilment of their desires or out of fear: "O Lord, grant me this desire!" Or "Please do not give me any of that!" Do such prayers not mean that they know better than God what is best for them, or, that they are, in short, greater than God? Do they really believe that God—who created both them and the world and who has protected both all along—does not know what is good and bad for them? They think that praying means presenting before God a litany of their likes and dislikes. Prayer is not an enumeration of one's personal desires.

This does not mean that we must not share our sorrows with God. We can certainly unburden our sorrows. Doing so will give the mind some relief. But more importantly, we must strive to remember God with love. Spend at least a little time every day meditating on God, chanting our mantra, and singing *bhajans* (devotional songs). If we go to temples, it should be to foster remembrance of God.

Do not think that we will receive God's grace just because we believe in him. We must act in accordance with our faith. We will not recover from an illness just because we believe in the doctor, will we? Likewise, faith and effort must go hand in hand.

Though God is within us, we are currently unable to experience His presence fully. But we can do so through devotion. Prayer, meditation and constant remembrance bind the mind strongly to God. Then, we will always be able to experience His presence.

Once, a man and his wife went on a cruise. Suddenly, the sky became dark. Thunder resounded and heavy rains started lashing down. Strong winds began to buffet the ship violently. Fearing for their lives, all the passengers started panicking. The man alone remained calm, in spite of all that was happening. But his wife began howling in terror. He tried calming her, but no matter how hard he tried, he could not. Finally, he became angry. He took a gun out from his bag, pointed it at his wife, and said, "Don't say another word. If you do, I'll kill you!"

Seeing the gun, the wife nonchalantly replied, "Do you really think you can intimidate me?"

The husband asked, "Don't you feel even the slightest fear at the sight of this gun?"

She said, "I know it's is a lethal weapon. But as long as it's in your dear hands, I've no fear. I know that you'll never hurt me."

The man said, "Likewise, I know that this strong wind is controlled by God, whom I worship. I have the firm faith that He will never harm me. That's why I'm able to face this grave danger fearlessly."

Children, once we become aware that any challenge in life is God's handiwork, we will be able to face any situation fearlessly. This does not mean that we should remain idle. We must do what needs to be done. But we must accept what we cannot change as God's will. If we can do that, we can live in this world peacefully.

47. Smile

Children, a sweet smile on the face is an outward expression of the divine consciousness within. Where there is a sincere smile, there one will always find love, happiness, compassion and patience. A smile brightens up our life. A sincere smile is like a light that dispels the darkness of sorrow and disappointment from the hearts of others.

A man was standing by the roadside, looking dejected. Rejected by everyone, he had lost the will to live. A small girl passing by gave him a sweet smile. That smile comforted him to no end. The thought that there was at least one person in the world who would smile at him revitalized him. He thought about a friend who had helped him years ago when he had been in trouble. He at once wrote a letter to his friend. When the friend received the letter from this man, whom he had not heard from for years, he was elated. He gave ₹10 to a poor man, who bought a lottery ticket with it. Wonder of wonders, his ticket won the jackpot! After he had claimed the prize money, he saw a sick beggar lying by the roadside. The man thought, "God blessed me with this money. Let me help this beggar." He took the beggar to the hospital and paid for the treatment.

After the beggar recovered and was discharged, he saw a puppy that had fallen into a puddle of water. The wet puppy was too frail to walk. It was whining pitiably from cold and hunger. The beggar picked it up, wrapped it in his own clothes, and carried him on his shoulders. He made a small fire to warm the shivering pup and shared his food with it. The food sated it and the fire warmed the puppy. Refreshed, it started following the beggar. When night fell, he went to a house and asked the owners if he could sleep there. They allowed him to spend the night in the outer veranda. In the middle of the night, all of them were awakened by the dog's ceaseless and frantic barking. They saw that one part of the house was up in flames: the room in which the only child in that family was sleeping. The parents rescued the child from the room and, by their collective efforts, were able to put out the fire before it spread any further. Giving the beggar and his puppy space to sleep had proven to be a blessing for the family.

It all started with the innocent smile of the small girl. All she did was to smile at a man on the roadside, but how many lives that smile touched! That smile was able to awaken love and compassion in the hearts of so many people and shine a light in their lives.

Even if we cannot help people in a big way, we must try to smile sincerely at those who are hurt and lonely and speak lovingly to them.

48. Lord Kṛṣṇa

Children, Lord Kṛṣṇa was a multi-faceted personality: He bequeathed to the world the *Bhagavad-Gītā*, re-established *dharma* (righteousness), and was an astute political strategist. But over and above everything else, he was the very embodiment of love, one who showered love on all.

Once, a scholar from Dwārakā reached Vṛndāvan. All the *gōpīs* (milkmaids) anxiously gathered around him, eager to hear news of the Lord. The scholar told them, "The Lord is leading a luxurious and happy life in Mathurā. It's a pity he did not take you there with him. He bestowed prosperity on Akrūra and Kucēla. He brought down the Kalpavṛkṣa (wish-fulfilling tree) from heaven for Satyabhāmā. Doesn't he know that you're still living in grass huts?"

When they heard this, the gōpīs said, "We're overjoyed to hear that the Lord is living happily. You pointed out that we're living in huts. When the Lord was a child, his tender footsteps graced all these huts, and therefore, they are more valuable than a palace for us. In our eyes, every single Kadamba tree in Vṛndāvan is a Kalpavṛkṣa. How many hallowed memories of the Lord these trees continue to give us! Remembrance of the Lord is the only wealth that is eternal and indestructible. Our only prayer is that those memories never leave us. For us, no palace or Kalpavṛkṣa is superior to these memories."

Seeing the gōpīs' innocent devotion, the scholar's eyes welled up with tears. He said, "When I received the Lord's darśan in

Dwārakā, I said, 'O Lord! My life has become fulfilled today.' The Lord said, 'You have seen only my body. To see my heart, you must go to Vṛndāvan.' Only now have I understood the meaning of his words. I have understood what real devotion is."

The minds of the gōpīs were always on Lord Kṛṣṇa, even amidst family responsibilities. They constantly chanted his name, whether they were churning yogurt, pounding grains or doing something else. They labelled the containers of condiments like chili and coriander with names like 'Kṛṣṇa' and 'Gōvinda.' While selling milk and butter, they did not ask, "Do you want some milk? Do you want some butter?" Instead, they called out, "Do you want Acyuta? Do you want Kēśava?" If we have innocent love, our mind will remain with the Lord even in the midst of our busy, mundane lives.

The gōpīs were neither too educated nor well-versed in the scriptures. Nevertheless, their innocent devotion to Kṛṣṇa gave them what the yōgis failed to gain even after ages of *tapas* (austerities). Such is the greatness of devotion.

Real devotion is self-surrender to the Lord, knowing that it is the One Lord who shines through all of creation and the different manifestations of divinity.

Remembering Lord Kṛṣṇa

Children, what are the first thoughts and words that come to mind when we think of Lord Kṛṣṇa? It is difficult to answer. People will give different answers because the Lord cannot be grasped by thoughts or concepts. But one thing is for sure: His divine play is sweet, enchanting and beautiful. The Lord loved peacock feathers, the flute, sandal paste and *tulasī* (basil) garlands. The allure of the peacock feather, the sweetness of the melody flowing from the flute, the cooling beauty of sandal paste, and the purity of the tulasī were not confined to Kṛṣṇa's form alone; they saturated his attitude and actions, too.

Poets sing Kṛṣṇa's infinite glories. He was an unequalled defender of dharma, canny political strategist, the dispenser of the magnificent *Gītā*, invincible opponent... all this is true. But more than all of this, Lord Kṛṣṇa was the very embodiment of love. He showered love on all. Not just the gōpīs and *gōpas* (cowherd boys), all creatures came under the spell of his love. In truth, the Lord incarnates for the sake of devotees, to awaken devotion for God in the hearts of people.

It is said that love has three phases. The first is the attitude of the pheasant. When it sees the moon, it forgets itself and stands transfixed, drinking in the moon's silvery rays to its heart's content. It has no other thought in its mind. Similarly, a true devotee will remain completely absorbed in thoughts of God.

The second phase can be compared to the pain of separation that the hornbill feels. It is always thirsting for rainwater. But even if its throat cracks or it is about to die from thirst, it will not drink water from ponds or wells. Only rainwater can slake its thirst. Similarly, a true devotee will have no desire at all for worldly pleasures, and will keep pleading with intense longing to attain God. This is a phase in the journey towards perfect devotion.

The third phase of love, illustrated by the moth, reveals the state of reunion following separation. When the moth sees the fire, it flies into it with blind enthusiasm. It sacrifices itself and becomes one with its beloved. There are no longer two distinct entities. There is no 'I.' However, the fire that the moths who were the gōpīs sought was the Lord, who is of the nature of immortality. There is no death when one is burnt by the blaze of immortality. One becomes immortal. Awaken love by remembering God, nourish it through separation from him, and become love by attaining oneness with him.

The Lord does not look at a devotee's position or prestige, caste or clan, or lineage, only at the purity of her heart. This is why the gōpīs of Vṛndāvan became most beloved to Kṛṣṇa. This is why he declined Duryōdhana's royal reception and slept in Vidura's humble home instead. This is why he perceived beauty in Kubjā, the ugly hunchback.

Rādhā's Kṛṣṇa

Children, it is difficult to describe Śrī Kṛṣṇa because he is beyond words and intelligence. He is the Truth from which speech and mind retreat, after they have failed to describe or understand It. He is knowledge, bliss and love, and yet beyond these. Śrī Kṛṣṇa was a divine incarnation whose life illumined the infinite glories of the Paramātmā (Supreme Self) in unparalleled ways.

It is usually said that God incarnates to protect dharma and to eliminate adharma. But a divine incarnation, especially Kṛṣṇa's, has an even greater aim: to awaken devotion in human hearts. A true devotee does not long even for *mōkṣa* (spiritual liberation). She has only one desire: to remember the Lord and to serve him. Lord Kṛṣṇa kindled this highest form of devotion in the gōpīs. His form, words, mischief and actions immersed them in bliss. There is no higher power or feat than love. That is why it is said that Kṛṣṇa's most glorious accomplishment was not the lifting up of the Gōvardhana Mountain but the awakening of this love in the gōpīs.

Once, the gōpīs asked Rādhā, "O Rādhā, the Lord, whom we loved and thought ours forever, has abandoned and orphaned us. Our existence has become meaningless. Why should we continue to live? Why did the Lord, who is the very epitome of love, behave so cruelly towards us?"

Rādhā replied, "Don't say that. The only one whom we can call our own for all time is the Lord. But he is not ours alone. He belongs to everyone. There are many people in this world who long to see the Lord and experience his love, whose longing is greater than ours."

Bending down to take a handful of water from the Yamunā, she said, "Look, the water will remain in my hands as long as they remain cupped. But if I close my fingers to seize the water for myself, I will lose whatever water I have. We tried to make the Lord ourselves alone and to imprison him in Vṛndāvan. He moved far away to help us understand that he dwells in the heart of every being. But though he left us, he never orphaned us. His every act was a divine play, and it has become a living memory within us. As long as we keep those memories alive, the Lord will be with us. He will dance forever by the river of love in the bower of our hearts."

Through their innocent devotion, the gōpīs quickly gained the Supreme Self, which the ancient sages attained only after performing austerities for ages.

Kṛṣṇa came to this world with a smile. He also bid farewell to this world with a smile. In contrast, we came to this world crying. At least while leaving, let us do so with a smile. May Kṛṣṇa's unfading smile become an inspiration. May love for Kṛṣṇa spread like radiant moonlight in the hearts of my children. May baby Kṛṣṇa frolic in our hearts forever.

Devotion of the Gōpīs

Children, quite a few spiritual teachers say that apart from the four goals of human life—dharma, artha (wealth), kāma (desire) and mōkṣa—there is a fifth goal: bhakti (devotion).

A true devotee does not even want mōkṣa. He has only one goal: to remember and serve God all the time. He does not want anything else. As far as he is concerned, bhakti is not for the sake of any other purpose. When devotion is for devotion's sake, the individual ceases to be and his surrender becomes total. Even then, the desire to relish devotion for God remains in his heart.

Thus, he constantly savors the bliss of devotion and becomes the very embodiment of bliss.

Once, Uddhava asked Kṛṣṇa, "I've heard that among all your devotees, the gōpīs are dearest to you. There are many others whose eyes also well up with tears at the mere mention of your name. They also slip into a meditative state as soon as they hear the melody of your flute. They forget their surroundings the moment they see your beautiful blue body, even from a distance. What is so special about the gōpīs that other devotees lack?"

Hearing the question, the Lord smiled and said, "All my devotees are dear to me. But there is something special about the gōpīs. The eyes of my other devotees well up when they hear my name. But the gōpīs hear any name as mine. For them, any sound is music issuing from my flute. In their eyes, every hue is blue. The gōpīs are thus able to see oneness in diversity. This is why they are dearest to me."

When a woman, for whom her husband is as dear her own life, picks up a pen to write a letter to him, she will think of him. As she takes the paper, her mind will be preoccupied solely with thoughts of him. Similarly, when a true devotee prepares for the *pūjā* (ceremonial worship)—when he gathers the trays, incense sticks, camphor tablets and flowers—his mind will be on God. At the height of devotion, the devotee beholds the Creator in all of creation. This was why the gōpīs did not see anything as separate from the Lord.

May the remembrance of Kṛṣṇa and the gōpīs of Vṛndāvan, who, forgetting everything else, danced blissfully and lived festively, fill our hearts with devotion, cheerfulness and bliss.

Servant of Devotees

Children, the aim of every divine incarnation is to awaken devotion in the hearts of people and thus purify their minds. This was also what Lord Kṛṣṇa aimed to do through his enchanting divine play.

Once during the Ōṇam[10] season, the gōpīs were playing on the swing with Lord Kṛṣṇa. After a while, the Lord said, "Let's enjoy the Ōṇam feast now. Go home and bring food to the banks of the Yamunā."

Hearing this, the gōpīs ran home and carried different items of food back to the riverbank. As Rādhā was hurrying with food to the Yamunā, she heard the sound of someone crying. It was a small girl sobbing inside a hut. She was asking her mother, "Why are we having *kañji* (rice gruel) at home even on Ōṇam? I don't want kañji. I want rice!"

The mother said helplessly, "Daughter, don't be difficult. Please eat the kañji. Your father is paralyzed. I need to attend to him and look after you as well. I begged all the neighbors for some grains, but did not get any. Tomorrow, I will somehow cook rice for you, daughter."

"That's what you said yesterday, too." Saying so, the girl started sobbing her heart out.

Hearing this, Rādhā's heart melted. She silently opened the door to the kitchen and quietly placed the food she had with her inside. She then removed her gold ornaments and put them beside the food items. Then, taking the vessel containing the kañji, Rādhā walked to the banks of the Yamunā.

By the time Rādhā arrived, all the other gōpīs were already seated around Lord Kṛṣṇa. They were waiting anxiously to see whose food the Lord would eat. Suddenly, feigning tiredness, He said, "I'm feeling feverish. I'd like some kañji. There's a vessel next to Rādhā. Please go and see what's inside that vessel." When he learnt that it contained kañji, the Lord eagerly drank

---

[10] Kerala's biggest festival, practically its national festival. It occurs in the month of *Cingam* (August – September).

from it. The others looked on, stunned. Kṛṣṇa looked at Rādhā and smiled sweetly at her. Rādhā's eyes overflowed with tears.

All the other gōpīs had taken the same route as Rādhā, but only Rādhā had heard the young girl's sobs. Rādhā's compassion moved the Lord. It is easy for anyone to love the Lord, but a true devotee is one who serves all, seeing the Lord in them. The Lord is willing to become the servant of such a devotee. Even if that devotee offers him a small leaf, he will accept it as if it were nectar.

Śrī Kṛṣṇa Jayanti

Children, people all over the world celebrate Aṣṭami-rōhiṇī (Lord Kṛṣṇa's birthday) with great joy. There are many lessons that people from all walks of life can learn and assimilate from the Lord's life.

Aṣṭami-rōhiṇī is the day Lord Kṛṣṇa was born to Vasudēva and Dēvakī, during the Dwāpara Yuga. That said, the Lord, who is without birth or death, lives on as pure consciousness, which is all-pervading. He must take birth in our womb of love.

The Lord was born with a smile, lived with a smile, and left his body with a smile. The message he conveys through Aṣṭami-rōhiṇī, his birthday, is to make our own lives blissful with laughter. We forget to smile or be happy while carrying the small burdens of life. Try cracking a joke with a man carrying a heavy load on his head. He will not be able to smile because of the heavy load. But look at Lord Kṛṣṇa. He shouldered responsibilities that were as heavy as the Himalayas, and yet, he never once forgot to smile. A *mahātmā* (spiritually illumined soul), he was engaged in so many spheres of activity, and he acted with utmost skill. He regarded each duty equally, and did not see one as superior to another, and discharged each perfectly.

Kṛṣṇa tasted defeat in war. He accepted defeat with a smile, and had no hesitation in doing so. Most people do not take responsibility for their failures but instead try to blame others. But if they win, they take all the credit for the success. But Lord Kṛṣṇa was not like that. He was bold enough to accept responsibility for defeat. No one other than him has set such an example.

Not to want to accept anything but success in life is a wrong attitude. We must also be able to welcome defeat. Life is not to be evaluated on the basis of the tally of victories and defeats. What is important is how we accept both. This is what the Lord's life teaches us.

Most people let even their small positions go to their head, and even forget that they are mortal beings. Yet, the Lord, though omnipotent, was never egoistic about his strength. When occasion demanded that he behave like an ordinary person, he became like an ordinary man among ordinary men. He was as patient as the earth. But when there was no other choice, he taught arch-egoists like Kamsa a good lesson.

In his life of ceaseless action, Kṛṣṇa joyfully donned all the different costumes that life demanded, and played all the roles to perfection. The costumes he wore included that of a king, subject, father, son, brother, classmate, warrior, messenger, Lord of the gōpīs, charioteer, the beloved of his devotees, and many others besides. He never did anything by halves. He removed the costumes only after he had finished playing all his roles.

Kṛṣṇa's life was like a cool breeze that gently caressed everyone and everything. He journeyed through life with the same ease as traveling from one room to another. He bestowed happiness liberally on all those who came into contact with him. He shuffled off his mortal coil only after blessing even the hunter whose arrow mortally wounded his foot.

May the memory of this blessed soul's blissful attitude towards life and his dexterity of action remain enshrined in everyone's hearts. May we all gain the strength and courage to follow in his hallowed footsteps.

49. Bhagavad-Gītā

Children, in ancient times, many *yajñas* (ritual sacrifices) were conducted in Kurukṣētra, where the Mahābhārata War was fought. In the *Mahābhārata*, the Kurukṣētra War is itself described in many places as a yajña. Kurukṣētra is the land of *dharma* (cosmic law) and *puṇya* (meritorious deeds). A *Kṣatriya's* (warrior's) *dharma* (duty) is to wage war. Kurukṣētra is also called Dharmakṣētra (field of dharma) as righteous deeds are performed there.

A righteous war was supposed to have been fought there but the Kauravas and Pāṇḍavas adhered to the conventions of war for only three days. Thereafter, both sides committed many atrocities. When there is growing contempt on both sides, most people feel like wounding and killing the enemy. This culminates in war. The Mahābhārata War ended when many who were sleeping at night were burnt to death. The law that an unarmed person should not be killed was breached. Such is the nature of war: once it starts, all sense of propriety and lawful conventions are violated. Children, war is never an answer to any problem. War and dharma can never coexist. Many of those who fought the Kurukṣētra War abandoned dharma during the battle.

It was through Sañjaya's eyes that Dhṛtarāṣṭra, the blind king, watched the Mahābhārata War being fought. Thanks to the power of clairvoyance that Sage Vyāsa bestowed on Sañjaya, the latter was able to relay to Dhṛtarāṣṭra how the war was unfolding in distant Kurukṣētra. At the start of the war, on Arjuna's request, Lord Kṛṣṇa steered the chariot to the middle of the battlefield, where the opposing forces were arrayed against each other. Seeing the warriors ranged on both sides, Arjuna's mental state became utterly pathetic. He saw only relatives and teachers on both sides, and became increasingly despondent. He thought, "I have to try and kill Bhīṣma, my venerable grandfather, and Drōṇa, my revered teacher. If I kill them all, which of my relatives will remain alive? I want neither victory nor the kingdom at the expense of their lives." Overcome by dejection, Arjuna cast aside his bow and arrows and slumped down in the chariot.

Lord Kṛṣṇa reminded Arjuna about the duties of a Kṣatriya. He did not treat the symptoms of Arjuna's depression; He worked directly on the latter's mind. Seeing the symptoms of depression in Arjuna, Lord Kṛṣṇa fed him the nectar of the *Gītā* (divine counsel) and thus freed him of the disease.

Children, you must read the *Gītā* not just with the head but with the heart as well. The *Gītā* was able to rouse Arjuna, who had even considered suicide, to valorous action. The *Gītā* is the ideal pathfinder for those who think of taking their own lives when the problems of life become unbearable. Many of Amma's Western children approach the *Gītā* with reverence and an inquiring mind, and find befitting answers to the problems besetting their lives in the pages of the *Gītā*. We must all follow this path.

It was not for Arjuna alone that Lord Kṛṣṇa stationed the chariot in between the two warring forces. His combatants included brilliant and formidable foes such as Bhīṣma, Karṇa and Drōṇa. The Lord stopped the chariot right in front of them. One of the meanings of the word 'Kṛṣṇa' is 'one who attracts.' Lord Kṛṣṇa, the Supreme Self, is he who attracts all beings in the universe to him. The Lord drew the brilliance and battle prowess of stalwarts such as Bhīṣma. When Bhīṣma came face to face with the Lord, he joined his palms in reverence. It was for Arjuna's sake that Kṛṣṇa drew the energy and power of these great warriors. It was also why Kṛṣṇa stopped the chariot in the center of the battlefield. Seeing the distress of his devotee, the Lord consoled him and nullified the virtuosity and valor of his enemies. Children, remember that the Lord will act in this way to protect the true devotee who has taken refuge in him. Pray to the Lord for complete self-surrender.

Message of the Gītā

Children, the Bhagavad-Gītā is the essence of all the Vēdas, which are as deep and as expansive as the ocean. However, people cannot drink seawater or use it for any other purpose at home. But when water from the ocean evaporates in the sun's heat, condenses as clouds, falls as rain, and flows as a river, it can quench everyone's thirst and be used for many other purposes besides. Likewise, the Bhagavad-Gītā is the spiritual Ganges flowing to us from the ocean of the Vēdas by divine grace.

The message of the *Gītā* is for the entire human race. It brings together the paths of devotion, knowledge and action and other spiritual principles. Lord Kṛṣṇa came to show people of different temperaments the way to attain the Supreme. If a restaurant serves only one dish, only those who like that dish will go to the restaurant, whereas food in a variety of tastes will draw everyone. Clothes in just one size will not fit everyone, whereas clothes in different sizes will attract people of all sizes. Similarly, the *Gītā* shows people from all walks of life diverse ways to spiritual enlightenment. The Lord's utterances gently guide and uplift each person from his or her level.

Some people accuse the *Gītā* of promoting war. The truth, however, is that it shows both the individual and society the way to peace. What the Lord is teaching us through the *Gītā* is how, when there is no other alternative, even war can become a *sādhana* (spiritual practice). When Dakṣa[11] performed a yajña, his arrogance caused the yajña to become a *yuddha* (war). But Arjuna, acting upon the Lord's advice, was able to transform a yuddha into a yajña by surrendering to the Lord. One of the most important messages of the *Gītā* is the secret of transforming *karma* (action) into *karma-yōga*, making action a means to God-realization.

The spirit of sectarianism or narrow-mindedness is completely absent from the *Gītā*. It does not ask us to worship a God sitting on a golden throne in the heavens above. Nor does it ask us to strive for a place in heaven after death. The *Gītā* shows us how we can experience supreme peace here and now. It exhorts us to realize the supreme truth, which inheres as our very own Self.

Though brief, the message of the *Gītā* is as deep and vast as the ocean. The *Gītā* is the very symbol of Sanātana Dharma.[12] It is the elixir that the Lord dispensed after churning the milk ocean of the Vēdas. The *Bhagavad-Gītā*, a manifestation of the Lord's enduring presence, will continue to bless this world forever.

[11] Mind-created son of Brahma, the Creator, and father-in-law of Lord Śiva. Out of contempt for the Lord, Dakṣa did not invite the Lord or his daughter, Satī (the Lord's consort), to the yajña he conducted. This culminated in a war.
[12] Literally, 'Eternal Law,' the original name of Hinduism.

50. Non-violence

Children, non-violence is the highest *dharma* (duty). Whether one is leading a spiritual or worldly life, one must try not to hurt any living being. The waves of pain arising from even the smallest being who is hurt create ripples in the atmosphere, and will adversely affect the one who hurt it. Therefore, do not hurt any creature in thought, word or deed.

That said, we must first understand correctly what violence and non-violence actually are. Violence is hurting others through indiscriminate or selfish action. But actions done with the intention of helping others cannot be considered violence.

What determines whether an action is violent or non-violent is the attitude behind it. Amma can give an example. A woman gave her maid, a young girl, a lot of work. Though she tried hard, the child could not finish her chores on time. The mistress scolded her, making her cry. The same woman spanked her daughter for neglecting her homework and playing instead. The daughter sat in a corner of the room and started crying.

Here, both children were crying. The mother's spanking of her child cannot be considered violence because she had spanked her daughter with a good intention: she wanted her daughter to have a bright future. This is not violence, only a reflection of her love for the child. That said, though the woman did not spank her maid, her behavior towards the girl was callous and violent. Would a mother treat her child this way? Here, we must consider the attitude behind the different treatments meted out to the two children.

While planting a fruit-bearing sapling, we might uproot many small plants around it. But when the sapling becomes a tree, how beneficial it will be to society! Not only that, many small plants can grow in its shade. Looked at from this perspective, uprooting the small plants was no loss and cannot be considered violence.

Even hurting a few individuals for the selfless purpose of safeguarding the well-being of society cannot be considered violence. This is why the Mahābhārata War is considered a righteous war. There are those who ask if the Lord was not abetting violence when he urged Arjuna to fight. The Lord never wanted war. His path was one of patience. He kept forgiving. He pleaded with Duryōdhana to give the Pāṇḍavas at least one hut. But Duryōdhana adamantly declared that he would not give them so much as a hair's breadth of land. If the patience of a strong man emboldens a person to be cruel or to harm people, then that patience is the worst violence. However, we should not harbor enmity or jealousy towards anyone. We must censure the wrongdoing, but not have any anger towards the wrong-doer.

Some people might wonder if it is possible to become totally non-violent in our actions. Even if we cannot rise up to that level, we must keep non-violence as our goal, and strive constantly to love and serve others.

51. Righteousness and Spirituality

Children, some people say, "We lead an ethical life. We do not betray or harm anyone. We don't steal either. We live happily, content with what we have. We don't see the need for spirituality or belief in God."

True, living an ethical life is important. Doing so is equally beneficial for the individual and society. But it may not be enough when one has to face life's challenges. If our actions are not rooted in discernment and wisdom, even minor setbacks and sorrows can make us lose our mental balance. That being the case, how can we bear bigger setbacks in life?

Many of us do good with expectations. Hence, we end up disappointed even after doing good deeds. Those we love sincerely might not reciprocate our love. Some people become disillusioned when their expectation of love is not fulfilled. They resort to intoxicants and eventually become addicted. Similarly, someone we have helped a great deal might betray us. We might then become terribly upset or angry and become obsessed with thoughts of revenge. The cause of all these is expectation. With spiritual knowledge, we can retain our mental balance in such situations.

Spirituality is the management of life. It teaches us how to live in this world and how to overcome challenges. If we understand the world and its nature, we will be able to face and overcome every challenge bravely.

Suppose we are going to see an old friend in order to borrow some money from him. He might or might not lend us the money. He might even say, "I was also thinking of borrowing some money from someone." If we keep these outcomes in mind, we will not get upset even if he does not lend us any money.

A ship in the ocean is surrounded by water. As long as the water does not seep into it, it is safe. But if a small hole appears anywhere in the ship, water will enter, causing the ship to sink. Similarly, if we allow the events of the outer world, whether good or bad, to influence our mind, it will become unsettled and enslaved by sorrow and disappointment. But if we surrender the mind to God, we will always remain calm.

For example, suppose a close friend dies in an accident or is seriously ill. In such a situation, how can we have peace of mind? It is the knowledge of spiritual principles and a life lived accordingly that will help us retain our mental balance.

During the 2001 earthquake in Gujarat, tens of thousands of people lost everything. Many of them had been poor to begin with. Quite a few of them came to see Amma. They were not overly distraught. When Amma asked them if they were upset, they said "God took back what He gave us." Though they lost everything, they were able to rise above their loss. What helped them to do so was their spiritual outlook.

All objects in the world are perishable. We can lose them any moment. Knowing this, we must take refuge in what is imperishable: God. If we anchor our lives in faith, we can survive the strongest storm.

52. Essence of Religions

Children, religions teach that God dwells in the heart, that man and God are essentially of the same nature, and that God created man in his own image. Many may wonder why, if such is the case, we are unable to savor the bliss of His presence. It is true that our true nature is divine but He remains hidden from us because of our ignorance and ego. Hence, we experience sorrow and suffering.

In reality, all religions show the ways by which man may attain his innate, blissful nature. However, failing to understand the real essence of religions, we get caught up in external rituals and customs. Suppose there is honey in different bottles. What is the point of giving all our attention to the color and shape of the bottles and not savoring the sweetness of the honey? We are like this at present. Instead of assimilating the principles that religions advocate, we have become caught up with their superficial aspects.

Amma remembers a story. A man decided to celebrate his 50th birthday with great fanfare. He printed invitations on expensive paper. He renovated his home by repainting and decorating it, and buying a chandelier, which he hung in the middle of the hall. He bought expensive clothes, a diamond ring and a gold chain to wear on his birthday. He also hired the most famous chef in town to cook up a sumptuous feast.

The birthday finally arrived. Wearing his designer clothes, diamond ring and gold chain, he went to receive the guests in the hall. The feast had been prepared, and uniformed waiters stood ready to serve. But when no one had arrived even after it turned dark, the man became anxious. Suddenly, he noticed the stack of invitations lying on his table. In the rush to renovate and do up his home and surroundings, he had completely forgotten about posting the invitations. Likewise, many of us get caught up in the trivial bustle of our daily lives, and forget the main aim of life. Hence, we are unable to experience true peace and happiness.

Those who are steeped in the outer pomp and pageantry of religion will find it difficult to assimilate the essence of religion and to experience the presence of God. The grass cutter who mows the lawn sees only grass, whereas the man collecting medicinal plants will notice the rare medicinal plants growing amidst the grass. In the same way, we must learn to absorb the cardinal principles of religion and not give too much importance to non-essential matters.

Children, we must strive to understand the inner essence of religion and the spiritual principles behind rituals and festivals. We must try to practice them in our lives. Only then will we be able to experience the presence of God within us.

53. Attitude

Children, many people in society lead despondent lives because of problems at work or other issues. The main reason for this is their attitude or faulty vision of life. If someone can guide them properly and inspire them, their lives will definitely change for the better. Through this positive transformation, those who were a burden even to themselves will become assets to society.

A college student had an intense desire to become a doctor. However, he failed the medical school entrance examination by one mark. He was sorely disappointed. He did not feel like enrolling in any other course. After some time, succumbing to pressure from family, he applied for a bank job and was successful. Even after he started working in the bank, the disappointment at not being able to become a doctor continued to haunt him. He was unable to speak politely to customers or even smile at them. Understanding his state of mind, his friend took him to see his Guru. The man opened up in front of the Guru and disclosed his problems: "My mind is not under my control. I get angry even over small matters. I'm unable to behave professionally to bank customers. I don't think I'll be able to keep this job much longer if I continue behaving like this. What should I do?"

The Guru consoled the young man and said, "Suppose your best friend sent someone to you. How would you receive him?"

"I will joyfully attend to all his needs."

"If so, consider each customer who comes to you as having been sent by God personally. You will then be able to interact with them lovingly."

Front that day onwards, a great transformation took place in the young man. The change in his attitude was reflected in his thoughts and actions. When he was able to see each person approaching him as an emissary of God, everything he did became an act of worship. Depression left him. His mind became filled with happiness and contentment. He was also able to spread his happiness to others.

Devotion is immensely helpful in fostering the right attitude in life. As far as a believer in God is concerned, the center of his life is God. He sees God in everyone and everything. All his actions are offerings to God. If we can do everything as an act of worship, we are not the only ones who will benefit from it; the whole of society will also benefit.

54. The Eternal and the Transient

Children, nothing that we see in this world is eternal. The property, wealth, relatives and friends whom we consider ours will not be with us for all time. This does not mean that we must not love anyone. We must love everyone but our love must be selfless. Only then can we be free of sorrow.

A man had four wives. Of the four, he loved his fourth wife the most. He did everything he could to provide her with the comforts of life and to support her healthy lifestyle and beauty regimen. He also loved his third wife dearly, and was proud of her extraordinary ability to get things done. As for his second wife, though he did not love her as much, it was only to her that he opened his heart and disclosed everything. He totally neglected his first wife; he did not so much as even look at her.

One day, he was diagnosed with a terminal disease. The doctor said, "Medical science cannot save you. You have only a few more days to live."

Hearing this, the man began to panic. When he reached home, he asked his fourth wife, "I loved you more than anyone else. The doctor says that I will die in a few days. Will you follow me beyond death?"

"No."

Her answer hurt him terribly. He asked his third wife, "Will you be with me after I die?"

"No, that's not possible. I want to continue living in this world. After you die, I'll marry someone else."

Hearing this, the man became sad. He asked his second wife, "In both joy and sorrow, I opened up my heart only to you. Will you follow me when I die?"

"I'll accompany you to the crematorium but no further."

Her words doubled his sorrow. As he sat there, terribly upset, his first wife consoled him: "You needn't worry at all. I'll always be with you. Never doubt it."

Hearing this, the man felt remorseful for having neglected her.

In this story, the fourth wife is our body, which will be with us only until our death. The third wife is our position, power and wealth. Once we die, someone else will claim them. The second wife is our friends, who will be by our side only until our body is taken to the crematorium. The first wife is our Self, which will be with us in life and death. But we never think of the Self, though it deserves the most attention from us.

This does not mean that property and wealth are not necessary. We only need enough to live. When we live with the understanding that the Self is the source of eternal peace, we can overcome sorrow.

55. Prārabdha

Children, many people ask, "I have not knowingly done any wrong in this life. Why then am I suffering so much?"

The only answer that can be given is that they are suffering because of evil deeds done in previous lives.

The consequences of actions done in previous lives and which we have begun to experience is called *prārabdha*. Some kinds of prārabdha give us sorrowful experiences whereas other kinds bestow pleasurable experiences.

There are three kinds of prārabdha. The first can be mitigated completely. It is like a disease that can be cured by taking medicine. The second kind of prārabdha is more severe, and is like a disease that can be healed only through surgery. The second kind of prārabdha can be mitigated through charitable acts, good deeds, and worship of God. The third kind of prārabdha is even more critical. One must experience it; there is no other way. It is like a disease that relapses even after surgery.

We must never give up optimistic faith. Some actions produce instant results whereas others produce results later. Sincere effort yields good results sooner or later. We should not become dejected, thinking that we have sinned in our past life. The past is like a cancelled check. Neither can it return nor can we change what we did in the past. Tomorrow can never become today either. All that we have is the present moment. We must use it well. Just as pouring fresh water continuously into salty water can reduce its salinity, we must do good deeds, thinking of the Supreme and offering our actions to him. In this way, we can reduce the intensity of sorrowful experiences and move ahead in life.

Once, a traveler crossing a dense forest was accosted by robbers. After stealing his money, the robbers bound his hands and feet with a rope, and threw him into a dry and disused well. The helpless traveler started shouting, "Save me! Save me!" Hearing his cries, another traveler went to the well. He threw a rope into the well and helped the first man climb out of the well.

The man was bound and saved by a rope. Actions are like a rope. Selfish actions bind us, whereas selfless actions dedicated to God lead to spiritual liberation.

We may not always have good experiences in life. Often, hardship awaits us. We must learn to use such occasions as stepping stones to our growth and success. To do so, we need to have discernment rooted in spiritual understanding.

56. Medicine of Love

Children, love is the sovereign remedy for mental impurities such as anger and jealousy. If we truly love someone, we will not feel jealousy, rivalry or hatred towards him. We will not perceive even his shortcomings as such. If the person we love is not beautiful, we will superimpose beauty on her. Conversely, even if the person we detest is beautiful, we will see her as ugly. The mind is behind both.

A housewife and her maid were cooking together in the kitchen. Looking out of the window, the housewife told her maid, "There's a fatso standing at the door. Please go and see who it is."

The servant went to see who it was. Returning, she said, "Madam, do you know who is standing outside? It's your eldest son, who left home 10 years ago!"

On hearing this, the woman ran outside, hugged the young man, and said, "Dear son, when did you return? Why have you become so thin? Aren't you eating well?"

The same person, whom the woman considered fat when he was a stranger to her, struck her as being slim when she recognized him as her son. When love awakens, ugliness turns to beauty. Through love, we can similarly rise above emotions such as jealousy and resentment.

Harboring anger towards another person is akin to suicide, because resentment and jealousy kill cells in the body. At the same time, when we love others, our mind becomes expansive and free of impurities. Good qualities and happiness naturally illumine a pure heart.

It is natural for us to feel sympathy when we see someone in a wheelchair. A person who cannot control his mind is likewise disabled. The only thing is, his disability is not visible outside. Just as we feel sorry for the disabled, we ought to likewise feel sorry for those who harbor feelings of hostility and jealousy. Perhaps, our love and sympathy might bring about a transformation in them.

Love and life are not two; they are one. Love and life are like a word and its meaning. It is not possible to separate them. A life without the sweetness of love is like a parched and fissured desert. Therefore, we must awaken love in our life. By doing so, we can help to maintain peace and prosperity not only in our life but in society as well.

57. Goal-orientedness

Children, it is rare to find someone who does not desire success in their lives. But very few people truly succeed in life. The others accept defeat, sink into despair, and lead despondent lives. The main reason for this is a lack of clarity about their goal and insufficient mental and physical preparation to attain it.

Many people who fail justify themselves thus: "The others had facilities that were conducive for success. They had people to help and encourage them. I had none of these." These excuses reveal their lack of *lakṣya-bōdha* (goal-orientedness) and weak will power. There is no use trying to hide our own weaknesses and laziness. In order to succeed in anything, we must have the will power and stamina to overcome obstacles in the way.

Students who want to become engineers or doctors, or top the class, study with lakṣya-bōdha. Their lives naturally become disciplined. They do not waste time hanging around with friends. They continue to study even while traveling in the bus. They will not complain about the lack of lighting at home but study under a street lamp. Circumstances do not deter the ones with lakṣya-bōdha, whereas for others, even a minor obstacle seems to be a big hurdle.

Once, a mother and her son went to a festival. There was a music-and-dance program in one corner of the festival grounds. Around this place were many stalls selling food, toys and other items. The child walked past all these, holding his mother's hand and avidly taking in the sights. For a few minutes, the mother forgot about the child. After a while, she realized that her son was missing. She looked around anxiously. She frantically searched for him in every nook and corner of the festival grounds. There was only one thought in her mind: "Where's my son?" She was oblivious to the music and dance around her. Nor did she notice the crowds or hubbub around her. Similarly, one who has lakṣya-bōdha will not entertain self-defeating thoughts or give in to obstacles.

First of all, we must develop a clear understanding of what we want to achieve in life. We must also strive constantly to attain the goal. If these two are in place, everything else will follow naturally. The petals of a flower fall away naturally when the plant is about to bear fruit. Likewise, when lakṣya-bōdha becomes firm, bad habits and weaknesses will naturally fall away. All the qualities needed to attain the goal will manifest gradually. Therefore, proper lakṣya-bōdha is of paramount importance.

58. Devotion and Contentment

Children, devotion is constant and unbroken remembrance of God. Take the *gōpīs* (milkmaids) of Vṛndāvan, for instance. They found it hard to let even a moment pass without thinking of Kṛṣṇa. In the kitchen, they labelled condiments like chili and coriander with names of the Lord. If they needed chili, they would say that they want Mukunda. When they took out coriander, they felt they were holding Gōvinda in their hands. Thus, no matter what they were doing, their minds were occupied with remembrance of God. Finally, they experienced Lord Kṛṣṇa's omnipresence.

When love for God fills the heart, all latent tendencies and desires that used to occupy the heart become weakened. Mental impurities leave. In this state of devotion, the devotee desires nothing other than God. Nothing else is important. The devotee accepts joy and sorrow as *prasād* (consecrated offerings) from God. He remains content even in poverty.

A king went hunting in the forest. While chasing animals, he lost his way and became separated from his retinue. There was a heavy downpour and the king was drenched to his skin. He wandered for a long time and became totally exhausted. When it was dusk, he saw an old Kṛṣṇa temple and a hut next to it. The king walked to the hut. An old priest and his wife were living there. Seeing the soaked and dripping stranger, they handed him a clean towel. After the king had dried himself, they offered him food. The king spent the night in the hut.

At dawn, the king's retinue of soldiers, who had spent the night searching for him, arrived at the hut. As he bade farewell to the couple, the king instructed that a hundred gold coins be given to the priest. The elderly man politely declined the offer and said, "We need nothing. The Lord is taking care of us. He gives us all that we need."

The king was amazed. He said, "Both of you are old. What if you fall sick? Let me build a new home for you. I'll also send someone to help you."

The elderly couple once again demurred. "We never think of disease. The Lord, who is Dhanvantari (Lord of Medicine), is always with us, protecting us."

Though they were poor, the faces of the elderly couple were bright with faith and contentment.

Simplicity and self-sacrifice come naturally to a true devotee. He does not think of his own safety or of personal interests. He receives all that life offers him—joys and sorrows, difficulties and gains—as God's prasād. He has no resentment, complaints or objections, only unflinching faith and love.

59. Open Mind

Children, we must always have the attitude of a beginner. This means having an open mind, being humble and having an avid desire to learn. It is the readiness to see and accept the good in anything. Approaching every situation in life with an open mind awakens patience, alertness and enthusiasm. We can learn lessons from any situation and respond appropriately. A closed mind makes one proud and obstinate, incites one to do wrong, and hinders the assimilation of goodness. Such an attitude eventually leads to self-destruction.

During the Mahābhārata War, Arjuna and Karṇa came face to face with each other one day. Lord Kṛṣṇa was Arjuna's charioteer, and Śalya, Karṇa's charioteer. Each warrior fired a fusillade of arrows at the other. Finally, Karṇa strung an arrow and aimed it at Arjuna's head, intending to finish him off. Śalya advised him, "Karṇa, if you're planning to kill Arjuna, don't aim the arrow at his head but at his neck."

Karṇa arrogantly retorted, "Once I string an arrow and take aim, I never alter my aim. Arjuna's head will remain the target of my arrow." So saying, Karṇa released the arrow. Seeing it whizzing towards Arjuna's head, the Lord pressed the chariot down with his foot, causing the wheels of the chariot to sink deep into the ground. Instead of striking Arjuna's head, the arrow knocked his crown off. Thus Arjuna was saved. Soon afterwards, he killed Karṇa. If Karṇa had followed Śalya's advice, the arrow would have struck Arjuna's head. Alas, Karṇa's ego did not allow him to heed Śalya's counsel with an open mind. Thus, Karṇa paved the way for his own death.

If we cling to a 'know-it-all' attitude, we will never learn anything. Can anything be poured into a full vessel? The bucket can be filled only when it is dipped into a well. Even a Nobel Prize-winning scientist must submit to a flute teacher if he wants to learn how to play the instrument.

A beginner's attitude is the doorway to the world of knowledge and expansive vision. One with this attitude feels, "I don't know anything. Please teach me." He or she will be humble and receptive. Such an attitude draws divine grace and helps one gain knowledge of anything. Thus, one can attain success in life.

60. Temple Darśan

Children, some people complain, "Though we have visited many temples and gone on many pilgrimages, our desires have yet to be fulfilled." Visiting temples and going on pilgrimages are all very well, but our aim should not just be to fulfil our desires. Our goals ought to be purifying the mind and awakening devotion to God. If we do not gain mental purity, all our spiritual endeavors will be in vain.

During construction, the concrete becomes set only if the steel rods used in construction are dirt free. Similarly, God can be enshrined only in a pure heart. While visiting temples and other sacred places, we must think of God and cultivate an attitude of surrender. We must spend our time there in chanting the Lord's names, singing bhajans, meditating or doing other spiritual practices. Even if our aim is desire fulfilment, the mind must be focused on God. But today, when most people go to temples, their minds are preoccupied with home, office and a hundred other matters. They tell God about all these and ask him to fulfil their desires. They cannot forget everything else and think only of him, even for a single moment. Once they have aired their sorrows, their minds return again to home or social matters. Some people wonder if the footwear they left outside the temple entrance might be taken away. Or the mind might run after the bus that takes them home. Before leaving the temple, they donate some money for the *vazhipāḍu* (ritual offering). After that, they will not linger there any more. They will say "bye" and leave.

This is not how it ought to be. We should try to spend all the time inside a temple thinking only of God. We must confide every detail to the lawyer or doctor. Only then can the lawyer fight our case properly; only then can the doctor treat our disease properly. But there is no need to tell God anything. He knows our heart. Therefore, meditate on the Lord and thus purify the mind. We must try to spend all our time in the temple chanting the Lord's name. Only then can we receive the full benefit of visiting the temple.

We will not make any spiritual or material progress by just going to the temple and circumambulating the shrine. No matter how many temples we visit, no matter how many offerings we make, visits to the temple will benefit us only if we turn our mind to God.

When it rains, water falls on the ground, turning it slushy and making it difficult for us to walk. The excess rainwater then flows away. In contrast, the oyster in the ocean might receive just one drop of rainwater, but nonetheless it transforms that single drop of water, for which it waited for a long time, into a precious pearl. Similarly, although God's grace is ever flowing, it will benefit us only to the extent we assimilate it.

61. Habits

Children, habits play an important role in our life. Good habits align our life in the right direction and lead us to success, whereas bad habits defile the mind and destroy life.

One who wants to enjoy complete freedom in life must ensure that he is not enslaved by habits. This goal is possible only with total awareness in each thought and action. If we keep repeating bad actions, they will become habits. Habit forms our character. Character controls us and we thus lose our freedom.

A man who has the habit of drinking coffee first thing in the morning becomes restless and irritable if he does not get it. Not getting even insignificant things like coffee, cigarettes and the newspaper on time can make the mind fidgety, and we become deprived of joy and contentment. We have all become enslaved by many such habits.

A man retired from the army after 30 years of service, and returned to his village. One day, he went to the market to buy a pot of milk. He placed the full pot on his head, held it there with both hands, and started walking home. Seeing him, one of the young men standing by the roadside shouted "Attention!" As soon as he heard the word, which had been part of his life for the last 30 years, the retired soldier instinctively dropped his hands to his sides and stood erect. The pot dropped and broke, and all the milk splashed out. The young men started hooting with laughter.

This story illustrates how even insignificant actions can be harmful if done mechanically. Such being the case, one can only imagine how destructive bad habits are.

Once we have become addicted to bad habits, it is difficult to overcome the addiction. To do so, we need to put in constant and conscious effort. By consciously cultivating good habits, we can avoid falling into the trap of bad habits and gain a noble personality.

That said, we must be careful not to let even good habits enslave us. Let us remember that good habits are for us; we are not for them. Suppose a man who always meditates at 8 a.m. has to take his brother who met with an accident to the hospital. His mind should not become unsettled just because he missed his meditation.

Someone who is learning how to swim will first use a life vest to stay afloat. Once he has learnt how to swim, he can dispense with it. Likewise, we must be able to overcome all habits gradually and thus experience total freedom.

62. Love Your Neighbor

Children, devotion to God is not only expressed through rituals or worship. It must manifest as love, compassion and patience towards fellow beings. As Jesus Christ advised, "Love thy neighbor as thyself." This advice has considerable spiritual and practical relevance. All of us love ourselves the most. But if we can see others as ourselves, our love will flow freely.

We believe that we are distinct individuals, but in truth, we are all fundamentally one. When love awakens, the sense of separateness dissolves, at least temporarily, and we experience oneness.

Our neighbors are the people we interact with in each and every moment of life. In that sense, family members, friends, colleagues and fellow travelers are all neighbors. If we can maintain good relations with them, it is we who will benefit. For many of us, loving our neighbors is not so easy. It is normal for human beings to find fault with others.

A newlywed couple started living in a new neighborhood. The next morning, they saw their neighbor hanging clothes out to dry. The wife told her husband, "She hasn't washed her dress properly. She probably doesn't know how to wash her clothes properly." The husband did not say anything to this. In the days that followed, the same thing continued to recur every morning, and the husband consistently refrained from responding to his wife's complaints.

After a few weeks, the wife pointed in great surprise to the clothes hanging on the washing line next door and told her husband, "Look, it seems our neighbor has finally learnt to wash her clothes properly. All the clothes on the line are really clean. I wonder who taught her how to wash her clothes!"

The husband replied, "I woke up early today and washed the dirt from our window panes."

This is exactly what happens in life, too. If we want to see goodness in others, we must first purify our own mind. Negative emotions such as arrogance, jealousy, envy and hatred distort our vision. As a result, we are unable to accept and love others.

By cultivating a loving attitude towards those we interact with, we can purify our own mind and create around us an atmosphere filled with love and happiness.

63. Is Anger Good or Bad?

Children, a small child once asked Amma, "O Amma, is there good anger and bad anger?"

What determines if an emotion is good or bad are the underlying reasons behind it and the benefit that emotion has. For example, a mother's show of anger for her child is meant for the child's good. There will not be the slightest trace of enmity or hatred for her child in the mother's heart. It is her love and affection for the child that is expressed as anger. It is similar to how a cat holds her kitten by the scruff of its neck while carrying it to a safe place. The mother only wants a bright future for her child. When she gets angry with the child, he might feel upset. But later, he will understand that his mother's anger had, in fact, saved him from grave danger.

A good teacher's scolding is like tutoring for a student. The teacher scolds only so that the student will study harder. Behind such anger, there is only love and affection. Here, the teacher wears anger like a mask, and the anger is another form of love. Hence, it will definitely help the student.

There is another kind of anger, one that is not aimed at anyone's welfare but arises from the arrogance and selfishness of the person who gets angry. An example would be the anger arising from the jealousy that a student feels towards another who has scored higher marks than he. Such anger will harm both, and must be contained at the outset. If we cannot do that, we must move away from the situation that provoked anger. It is natural for angry thoughts to arise in the mind. But we should not act under the influence of that emotion. Instead, we must distance ourselves from the situation that provoked our anger and reflect upon it. We must see to it that our anger does not translate into actions we will regret later.

How many family relationships and friendships have been broken by just one moment of anger! To a large extent, such problems can be avoided if both sides strive to restrain their anger and act with discernment. Meditating and doing other spiritual practices daily will help us to gain control over the mind. Gradually, we will be able to notice the very first thought of anger arising and thus control it. May each thought, word and deed of my children become meditative.

64. Mahātmās

Children, when a drama is enacted on stage, the audience will experience a range of emotions. They will laugh or cry depending on how the characters act. But what about the playwright watching his own play? He will not be anxious about the next scene. The playwright knows exactly what will happen next and what the characters will say. This is also how *mahātmās* (spiritually illumined souls) live in this world. They know what is happening and what is going to happen. Therefore, nothing in life can upset them.

Though mahātmās work constantly, they have no sense of being doers. They are not attached to their actions. They live in the world like butter floating on water. Children, remember what Lord Kṛṣṇa told Arjuna: "O Arjuna, I have nothing left to gain in the three worlds. Yet, I work." Some children might ask, "Why then do mahātmās act?" They act in order to awaken *dharma-bōdha* (consciousness of righteousness) in others. This is the aim of all their actions. Dharma will prevail only if *adharma* (unrighteousness) declines.

If a country is not protected from a depraved and cruel ruler, both the country and its people will be destroyed. When radiation is carried out to destroy cancerous cells, some good cells will also be killed. Nevertheless, this helps to heal the patient. Similarly, executing a man who will not hesitate to kill a hundred people can liberate a country and its people from the grip of adharma.

During the Mahābhārata War, Duryōdhana set out one night to see his mother, Gāndhārī. He was going to seek her blessings in order to win the war and to make himself invincible. Gāndhārī was a gem of a woman. She had blindfolded herself (as an act of solidarity) after marrying a blind man. As a result of the spiritual powers gained from this asceticism, the body of whomsoever Gāndhārī's gaze fell upon would become as strong as steel and he would become invincible. Duryōdhana knew this. In accordance with his mother's instructions, he bathed and was going stark naked to his mother when, suddenly, Lord Kṛṣṇa appeared before him and asked, "Duryōdhana, what are you doing? Going naked to your mother? Can't you at least wear a loincloth?"

Duryōdhana felt that the Lord was reasonable. He covered his groin and thighs and went to Gāndhārī, who removed her blindfold and gazed at her son. Every part of Duryōdhana's body that she gazed on became stronger than steel. Only those body parts that were covered remained vulnerable. Later, when Bhīma and Duryōdhana used maces to fight with each other, Bhīma was unable to defeat him despite repeated attempts. Finally, taking a hint from Lord Kṛṣṇa, Bhīma smashed Duryōdhana's thighs with the mace and thus killed him.

Some people consider this act of Lord Kṛṣṇa adharmic. However, he knew that if the evil Duryōdhana became invincible, dharma would not prevail in the kingdom. This is why he persuaded Duryōdhana to cover his groin and thighs. It was only because of this that Bhīma was able to defeat him. The actions of mahātmās might seem unethical to ordinary people. But we must not evaluate them based on a superficial reading of situations. We must evaluate the greatness of mahātmās only by taking into account the consequences of their actions.

65. Nothing is Insignificant

Children, nothing in this universe is insignificant. Everything has its place and importance. A failure to see this truth is the cause of most problems in life.

Negligence in small matters leads to huge losses. If a tiny screw becomes loose, the aircraft will malfunction and the lives of passengers will be in danger. Therefore, we cannot consider anything insignificant. Just because the problem is small does not mean that it is insignificant. If we give it due attention, we can avoid bigger dangers.

It is the attentiveness and patience we devote to small things that lead to big successes. Once, there was a doctor. Both age and experience had bestowed maturity on him. One day, a junior doctor called him agitatedly and said, "Sir, a patient has been brought in. He somehow swallowed a small ball. It's stuck in his throat. He's gasping for breath and is about to die. I've no idea what to do. Please tell me how to save the patient!"

After a few moments of silence, the senior doctor said, "Take a feather and start tickling him."

A few minutes later, the junior doctor called and excitedly said, "Sir, when I tickled him, the patient burst out laughing and the ball was ejected. It was truly a miracle! Where did you gain this knowledge?"

The senior doctor said, "When I heard about the patient's condition, this idea came to mind, that's all."

Just as a seemingly small and insignificant feather could save a man's life, we can accomplish great things by paying attention to small matters.

It is the attention and discernment that we show in seemingly insignificant matters that take us nearer to God. Attentiveness in outer matters leads to inner alertness. We need this in order to succeed in both spiritual and worldly life. Therefore, children, pay attention to everything.

66. Knowledge and Observances

Children, spirituality is the science of life. Through spiritual knowledge, we will be able to face each situation in life with the right attitude, and gain the strength to overcome challenges, crises and weaknesses. It is not enough to learn many spiritual principles, give talks, and advise others. Those principles must become part of our life. They must express themselves in our actions. The way we look at others, the way we walk, the way we sit, and the way we behave—all these should reflect spiritual knowledge. Students generally sit for examinations scheduled to take place at a certain date and time. But the true test of a student's caliber is in how he performs on a pop quiz.

Amma remembers a story. A cohort of students in a Gurukula[13] had completed their education. In order to obtain the certificate, they had to pass one more examination conducted by the Guru. As the students were hurrying to the Guru's hermitage to take the final exam, they passed a narrow lane strewn with thorns. Some of the students cursed their fate and stepped over the thorns. Others kept to the side of the lane, taking care not to step on the thorns. But one humble student told the others, "These thorns might prick the feet of people passing this way. It is still bright now but dusk will soon set in. Once it is dark, it will be difficult to find the thorns. If all of us work together, we can clear away the thorns in no time."

[13] Literally, the clan (*kula*) of the preceptor (*Guru*); traditional school where students would stay with the Guru for the entire duration of their scriptural studies.

But no one was willing to help. "The exam is going to start soon. If we're late, the Guru will be displeased. We need to reach his hermitage soon." Saying so, the students hurried away.

The lone disciple started picking up and throwing away the thorns. He did not stop even when the thorns pricked his hands. As soon as he had cleared the last thorn, he felt someone raising him up by his shoulders. It was the Guru. He hugged the disciple warmly and said, "It was I who scattered the thorns on this road to test all of you. You are the only student who passed the test!"

What is the essence of this story? The other students were more concerned with the kind of questions that the Guru might ask and with the answers to those questions. Their learning had not illumined their lives. But this disciple had transformed his life with the knowledge he acquired. The core of spirituality lies in putting others before oneself instead of being concerned with 'I' and 'mine,' and thus gaining a more expansive heart. One begins to see the problems of others and to feel their pain as one's own. In truth, by removing the thorns from another's path, one is really spreading flowers on one's own path. One need not pave one's path with flowers; nature herself will do so. It is not through words that a good disciple answers the Guru's questions but through his life. Hence, his negative tendencies and selfishness will fall away. It is only when the outer shell of the ego breaks open that we can find the true 'I' within. Once we find the true 'I,' we will see the Self in everything. Our life will thus become fulfilled.

67. Religious Intolerance

Once, a celebrated painter drew a portrait of a beautiful young woman. All those who saw the painting were captivated by her beauty. A few of them asked the painter if she was his girlfriend. When he said that she was not, they all wanted to possess her. They pressured the painter to reveal where she lived. The painter said, "Look, I've never even seen her before. The beauty you see in this portrait does not belong to any one individual. The picture is a composite of eyes, noses and other physical features of people I have seen. Even if you search the whole world, you will never find this woman."

But they did not believe him and angrily retorted, "You're lying! This is a tactic you're using to make her your own."

The painter once again tried to make them understand, but his efforts were in vain. Their desire to possess the young woman became even stronger. Each one of them declared, "I want her for myself. I shall make her my own!" This culminated in a brawl in which each attacked the other with weapons. Eventually, all of them were killed.

Believers today are like the admirers who wanted to make the young woman in the portrait their own. They strive to find God through the paths prescribed by their religious texts. They blindly believe that their God and their way alone are true. But God is the formless truth. There are many ways to attain him. Instead of understanding this, they fight and compete with each other, but never find God.

Each one of us sees the world through different colored lenses. If we look through the lens of hatred and sectarianism, we will see only enemies everywhere. We will never be able to see human beings as human beings. But if we look at the world through the lens of love and compassion, we will be able to see divine love and beauty pervading the entire universe.

Amma feels that if there is any religion that teaches its believers to see adherents of other faiths and devotees of other gods as devils, it is not a true religion but bigotry. In truth, the fundamental principles of all religions are love, compassion and unity. We must strive to assimilate these principles in our life.

68. Real Prayer

Children, prayer is the best spiritual practice for opening the heart to God and creating an emotional bond with him. It is like a bridge connecting the *jīvātmā* (individual self) and *paramātmā* (supreme self). When a young child returns home from school, he throws down his school bag, runs to his mother, and enthusiastically tells her about what happened in school, the stories his teacher told, and the sights he saw on his way back home. In the same way, prayer helps to cultivate a heartfelt relationship with God. Telling him everything helps us unburden our heart.

We must cultivate the attitude that God is our sole refuge. We must consider him our best friend, one who is always with us, in need and otherwise. When we open our heart to God, we unknowingly soar to the peaks of devotion. But not many people today have understood this benefit of prayer. For many, prayer means begging for the fulfilment of desires. This is not loving God. It is loving the objects of our desire.

Nowadays, there are people who even pray that others be harmed. A devotee should never think of hurting others. "God, may I do no wrong. Please give me the strength to forgive others for the wrong they do. Forgive me for my sins. Please bless everyone with goodness." Such ought to be our prayer. Praying like this gives us peace. The vibrations issuing from such prayers can even purify the atmosphere. A pure atmosphere has a benign effect on the lives of people.

The ideal prayer is one for the welfare of the world. Selfless prayer is the need of the hour. When we pluck a flower for *pūjā* (worship), knowingly or unknowingly, we are the first to savor its beauty and fragrance. When we pray for the well-being of the world, our heart becomes expansive. Our prayers also benefit the world.

Just as a candle melts while giving light to others, a true devotee longs to make personal sacrifices in order to help others. Their goal is to gain a mind that is willing to forget personal difficulties in a bid to make others happy. That is true prayer. People with such minds need not go anywhere in search of God. God will come in search of them. God will always be with them as succor and strength.

69. Real Prayer 2

Children, some people ask if praying and singing bhajans are not a mere display of emotion or weakness. Prayer and bhajans are not at all symptoms of mental weakness. They are not a mere display but a practical means to unburden the mind and awaken the heart. Just as opening the valve of a pressure cooker releases steam, prayer is a scientific means to reduce inner conflict and pressure.

Real prayer is a heart-to-heart dialogue between God and devotee. In such communion, the devotee experiences bliss every moment. When two people who love each other deeply talk to each other, they will not feel bored in the least, no matter how long they converse with each other. They will never feel that their conversation is a mere act.

Prayer is actually a dialogue with the inner lover. More than that, it is being able to distinguish the eternal from the ephemeral. The essence of prayer is this: "You are the Supreme Self, the *Paramātmā*, not the individual self, the *jīvātmā*. You are not meant to grieve at all, as bliss is your very nature."

Through devotion, we are not searching for a God in the heavens but striving to see divinity in everything, moving and unmoving. A devotee does not wander about in search of God. The purpose of prayer is to help him realize God, who shines within as eternal light.

When a hundred-watt bulb in the kitchen becomes coated with soot, its light will be even dimmer than that of a zero-watt bulb.

But if we wipe the soot away, the bulb will once again radiate bright light. Similarly, prayer is a means of getting rid of the mental impurities that veil our inner divinity.

Like the path of knowledge, the path of devotion also takes one to the experience of Self-realization. A child was bringing medicine to his sick and bedridden father. Just as he reached his father's bedroom, the lights went out suddenly. He could not see anything. The child touched the wall and thought, "No, not this." He touched the door and thought, "No, not this." He touched the table and thought, "No, not this." He felt the bed and thought, "No, not this." Finally, he touched his father and thought, "Dad!" He had reached his dad through a process of negation. Devotion is just like this. The devotee does not accept anything other than God. He thinks only of God. Whereas seekers following the path of knowledge say, "I am not the body, mind or intellect but the Self," the devotee says, "I belong to God. He has manifested as the whole of creation."

Through prayer, we gain the insight that everything is God. The devotee who sees God everywhere forgets himself. He loses his limited individuality completely and becomes one with God. His very life becomes a prayer.

70. Mental Worship

Children, some people worship the formless God. Others worship God in idols and other symbolic forms. The goal of both kinds of worship is to fix the mind upon God. It is hard for the mind to concentrate for even a moment. *Mānasa-pūjā*, or worship performed mentally, is the easiest way to tether the restless mind to God without relying on any external means.

The mind has a knack for identifying itself with whatever it thinks of. It is this knack that is being harnessed during mānasa-pūjā. This is why it is easier to gain one-pointed concentration during mānasa-pūjā rather than in ordinary *pūjā* (ritual worship). In mānasa-pūjā, we must first visualize our beloved deity sitting on a throne in the heart. Just as a mother bathes her child, dries her, dresses her, combs her hair, adorns her forehead with a mark, and prepares her for school, we must imagine worshipping our beloved deity with due pomp and pageantry. We must then chant the names of God or pray to our beloved deity.

The Lord is not concerned with the grandeur of the pūjā. What He wants is a heart full of surrender. He is satisfied only with such a heart.

Amma remembers a story. Once, a priest worshipped God with many types of flowers. He then asked, "O Lord, are You satisfied? Is there any other offering I should make?"

The priest was feeling proud, thinking that he had done something great and that he had made every possible offering. The Lord said, "There is one more flower that needs to be offered."

"Which flower is that?" the priest asked.

"The heart flower," replied the Lord.

"O Lord, where can I find that flower?" the priest asked.

"Near you," the Lord said.

He was referring to the flower that was the heart. But not understanding this, the priest started searching for a heart flower. He searched far and wide but did not find it. Finally, he fell at the Lord's feet and said, "O Lord, I couldn't find the heart flower anywhere. I have only my heart to offer. Please be content with this offering."

The Lord said, "This is the heart flower I mentioned. I love the flower of innocence the most. Even if you spend many millions of rupees and perform hundreds of pūjās, you will not experience my presence for even a moment. It is your innocent heart that I want, not your pūjās or wealth."

The goal of all spiritual practices is to develop one-pointed concentration on God. Mānasa-pūjā can help us develop such concentration easily.

71. Live in the Present Moment

Children, the mind rarely stays in the present moment. It is usually thinking about bygone events or those yet to come. All that we have is the present moment. It is like money in our hands. We can either spend it wisely or foolishly.

The pains, sorrows and guilt of the past often trouble us. Brooding over the past is akin to hugging a decomposed corpse. Conversely, if we keep thinking about the future, we will not be able to enjoy the peace and contentment of the present moment. One who settles down to sleep near a cobra's burrow will not be able to close his eyes peacefully for even a moment because of fear. Similarly, fears and anxieties about the future deprive the mind of peace. They will cripple whatever talent we have. Some children dance with great feeling while at home but are seized by fear when performing on stage, and end up moving like dancers on a wobbly stage. They will not be able to express any facial emotion. The fear inside will destroy the emotive beauty of the dance.

Living in the present means acting wisely in each moment without worrying about the past or future. It is the attentiveness with which we act in the present moment that determines how bright our future will be. Therefore, every moment is precious.

There was a boy who used to spend all his time watching television. Whenever his parents told him to study, he would say, "Examinations are in the future, aren't they? The wise say that one should not worry about the future but be happy in the present moment. I hate studying. I am watching TV so that I can remain happy in the present moment."

His parents took the boy to a Guru, who said, "Son, living in the present moment means making the most effective use of the present moment. If you do so, you will be able to live happily always. But if you waste your time on fleeting pleasures, you will regret it for the rest of your life. If you watch TV all the time, you won't even be able to earn enough money to buy a TV. Therefore, you must use each moment carefully. It is the present that shapes and safeguards the future. While studying, concentrate on your studies. While playing, enjoy the game. While praying, pray with all sincerity."

The present is an invaluable gift from God. If we act with alertness in the present, we will have a bright future.

72. Life is a Training Ground

Children, we all want others to behave lovingly and patiently to us. If we feel that their behavior is anything less than that, we will not hesitate to criticize, scold and judge them harshly. But many of us forget that others likewise expect dignified and exemplary behavior from us.

If we are caught in a traffic jam, we will honk continuously to make the car in front of us move ahead. We will curse the driver, as if he was the cause in the holdup. At the same time, we tell the driver behind us, "Hey, why so impatient? Can't you see the traffic jam? Please be patient."

Life is a training ground for us to improve ourselves. When we see someone doing wrong, we must learn not to make the same mistake ourselves. Similarly, when we see someone doing good, we must aspire to behave like that person and strive to do good. Cultivating such attitudes will help us improve and grow.

Most of us are not prepared to be truthful but can never forgive dishonesty in others. A thief waves a knife threateningly at a householder and says, "Where have you kept your gold and other ornaments and cash? Tell me the truth or I'll kill you!" Even a thief expects the truth from others.

Once, a man told a social worker, "I want to be a social worker like you."

The social worker said, "It's not so easy. You will have to make many sacrifices. You must be ready to give what's yours to the poor."

"I'm ready to undergo any sacrifice."

"If you have two cars, you must be ready to donate one."

"Why not? Certainly!"

"If you have two houses, you must give one away."

"Sure."

"If you have two cows, you must give one away to someone who doesn't have any cattle."

"Oh! I can't do that."

"Why not? You've no hesitation giving away a car and house. Why are you hesitating to give your cow away?"

"That's because I don't have two cars or two houses, but I do have two cows."

There is no space for idealism in a selfish mind. Idealism will be reflected in every thought, word and deed of one who has succeeded in conquering selfishness. More than any preaching, it is our practice of the ideal that will help others assimilate it.

73. Necessity of a Guru

Children, the scriptures say that God is within us, and that He is not separate from us. If so, some people might wonder why a Guru is necessary. God is within us, but to realize this, we must rely on a Guru to eliminate the ego in us. Only someone who is awake can awaken someone who is in deep sleep. Even though a wick contains all that is necessary to light it, we still need a flaming wick to light it. Similarly, in order to realize God within us, we need the help of a spiritually enlightened master.

If we dig for a well in certain places, we will never be able to find water no matter how deep we dig. But if we dig near a river, we will hit water after just a bit of digging. Likewise, the disciple's noble qualities and talents will soon manifest in the Guru's presence.

The Guru will create various situations to help the disciple get rid of his laziness, overcome his *vāsanās* (latent tendencies), and enable him to realize the Truth. Once, a Guru and his disciple were returning back to their āśram after a pilgrimage. Half way through the journey, the disciple said, "O Guru, I cannot take even one step further! Let me rest under this banyan tree for a while." The master insisted that they continue, but the disciple refused. The master continued his journey alone. He saw some people working in a field by the roadside. Their children were playing nearby. A baby was fast asleep on the ground. Without their noticing, the Guru picked up the baby and placed it next to his disciple, who was sleeping under the tree. The Guru then hid himself.

When the workers noticed that the baby was missing, there was chaos! They started running hither and thither in search of the baby. Hearing the commotion, the disciple woke up. The workers angrily asked him, "Did you steal our baby?" and were about to pounce on him. The disciple jumped up and ran for life, soon reaching the āśram. The Guru walked at a leisurely pace, and when he reached the āśram, he found the disciple sleeping in exhaustion. The Guru asked him, "You said that you couldn't take even one more step. But you reached the āśram before me." When the disciple is reluctant to obey the Guru's words, he will do anything it takes to bring him back to the right path.

Today, we are slaves to our mind and sense organs. But if we obey the Guru's instructions, we will be free from this slavery forever.

The Guru's Presence

Children, is a Guru needed to attain the spiritual goal? Many people wonder if obedience to the Guru is enslavement. We are now like the king who is grieving because he dreamt that he was a beggar. The Guru awakens us from the sleep of ignorance that causes sorrow.

If someone prompts us with the first line of a poem we learnt by heart in childhood but have since forgotten, the memory of the other lines will come rushing back. Similarly, we are in a state of spiritual oblivion. The Guru's advice has the power to awaken us from this forgetfulness.

There is a tree within the seed, but it will come into being only if the seed goes under the soil and its seed coat breaks open. Similarly, even though we are manifestations of the supreme truth, we will realize it only if the shell of our ego breaks open. The Guru will create circumstances to crush the ego. A plant can grow into a tree only if the weather is conducive, if it receives sufficient water and fertilizer at the right time, and if it is protected from pests and insects. The Guru likewise creates circumstances that are conducive for the disciple's spiritual growth. He will protect the disciple at all times.

Like a water filter, the Guru purifies our mind and removes our ego. We remain enslaved to the ego in every situation and do not act with discernment. Once, a thief entered a house, and the people staying there woke up. The thief fled, and the householders started shouting, "There goes the thief! Catch him!" The locals started running after the thief. As their numbers swelled, the thief joined the crowd and started shouting like them: "There goes the thief! Catch him!" As a result, no one could identify or catch him. Similarly, when the ego within rears its head, the disciple cannot perceive or stop it by his own power. He must submit to a Guru.

The Guru is striving constantly to uproot completely the 'I' sense in the disciple. Obeying the words of the Guru is not enslavement but the way to eternal freedom and everlasting bliss. The Guru has only one goal: to free the disciple from sorrow. The disciple might feel upset when the Guru scolds him, but he must remember that the Guru does so only to eliminate his vāsanās and to awaken him to his real nature. It will hurt a little when the vāsanās are being uprooted. To heal an infected wound, the pus must first be squeezed out. The doctor might even have to perform an incision to drain the wound. We might feel that the doctor is being cruel. But if, out of sympathy for the patient, he just applies medicine on the wound without squeezing the pus out, it will not heal. Likewise, the Guru's rebukes might hurt the disciple. However, the sole aim of the Guru is to weaken the disciple's vāsanās.

The Guru is not just an individual but the Supreme. He is the embodiment of ideals such as truth, *dharma* (righteousness), renunciation and love. In his presence, the disciple can assimilate these ideals and uplift himself. Such is the greatness of his presence.

The Real Guru

Children, among human relationships, the noblest is that between Guru and disciple. It occupies the highest place in Indian culture. But many today have not correctly understood this relationship. Some people ask, "Isn't obedience and humility to a Guru a form of enslavement?" In order to realize the Truth, the 'I' sense must go. It will be difficult for the disciple to eradicate that sense through spiritual practice alone. He must do spiritual practices under the Guru's guidance. By bowing his head down before the Guru, the disciple is paying homage not to the individual but to the ideal he embodies.

Obeying and respecting our parents, teachers and elders help us grow. Similarly, by obeying the Guru, the disciple becomes more expansive.

The Guru might be stern with the disciple but it is only for his own good. If a child tries to put its hands into fire, the mother might even spank him. Does she do it out of hatred? Never. It is only to save the child from danger. If a real Guru scolds his disciples, it is only because he has the disciple's spiritual progress at heart.

While traveling in an airplane, we have to wear the seat belt. This is not meant to curb our independence but to ensure our safety. Similarly, the Guru advises the disciple to practice *yamas* and *niyamas* (ethical precepts) and other rules only for his spiritual growth. They will protect the disciple from dangers.

If someone sees a man cutting sheets of color paper into pieces, he might ask, "Why are you tearing up these colorful sheets and wasting them?" not knowing that he is actually an artist making paper flowers. The artist sees something in those pieces of paper that others cannot see. Likewise, the Guru sees in the disciple something that he himself cannot see. The Guru behaves sternly and scolds the disciple only to help him manifest the Self within.

It is our attitude that makes any experience painful or joyful. The thought of the child to be born after 10 months makes pregnancy a joyous experience for the expectant mother. Similarly, a disciple who is mindful of his spiritual goal never considers the Guru's scolding or punishment a harassment.

A true master never sees his disciple as a slave. A Guru's heart is filled with love for his disciple. He longs to see the disciple succeeding, even if it means his own defeat. A true master is superior even to the noblest mother.

The Guru's Disciplining

Children, in spiritual life, considerable importance is given to the nearness of the Guru and to his disciplining. The Guru's presence and words will bring out noble qualities like patience in the disciple, even without his noticing. The Guru will guide him through situations that will bring out those qualities. He will make him do work that he dislikes. The disciple might disobey. The Guru will then counsel him, and his words will inspire the disciple to reflect upon those words. He will find the inner strength to overcome challenging situations.

Love is the most potent purifier of the human heart. Only the Guru's love is totally unselfish. Even if the whole world hates someone, his Guru will not. He will never abandon him.

Once, a Guru adopted an orphan and raised him lovingly. The other disciples felt that he was lavishing too much love and affection on the orphan. They became jealous. As he grew up, the adopted child developed bad habits and soon became addicted to many vices. Even then, the Guru's love for him did not lessen. The other disciples could no longer tolerate this. They just could not understand why the Guru was showing so much love to the rogue. One night, a disciple told the Guru, "Your darling son passed out after drinking and is lying in the street."

Without saying a word, the Guru set out from the āśram. After walking for some distance, the Guru saw the boy lying unconscious by the roadside in the freezing snow. He was not even wearing warm clothes. The Guru removed his woolen shawl, covered the disciple with it, and returned to the āśram. Early next morning, the disciple became conscious. When he noticed the shawl covering him, the disciple was mortified: "It's my Guru's shawl!" Overcome by remorse, he started crying and ran back to the āśram. He fell prostrate at the Guru's feet and washed his feet with tears. Those tears also cleansed his heart. A transformation took place in the boy, who had been despised by all. He even went on to become a role model to the other disciples.

The Guru, who knows the *samskāra* (mental impressions or personality traits) of his disciples, acts according to his divine intuition. Therefore, before we evaluate the Guru's actions, we must first recognize our own limitations. The Guru knows what is needed for the disciple's growth and acts accordingly. He leads the disciple to the goal by making him aware, at each moment, of the greatness of life.

The Guru's Greatness

Children, some people ask, "If the Guru and God are within us, why do we need an outer Guru?" It is indeed true that both the Guru and God are within us. However, most people are not independently capable of realizing the God within or assimilating the instructions of the inner Guru. Except for a rare few, who were born with a lofty spiritual predisposition gained from previous births, it is not possible for anyone to realize the Truth without the help of a Satguru in human form. The Satguru is a visible manifestation of God. But a Satguru's place is higher than that of God even, for it is the Guru who guides the disciple, who is bound by innumerable weaknesses and latent tendencies, with utmost patience and compassion.

The sculptor sees with his mind's eye the statue hidden inside the rock. The statue is revealed when he chisels away the unwanted portions. In the same way, the Guru brings out the pure essence of divinity concealed within the disciple. When the disciple performs spiritual practices in accordance with the Guru's instructions, his impurities vanish and the Truth stands revealed. It is akin to what will happen if we place a wax-covered statue near fire: the wax will melt, revealing the statue.

At present, even when we say that we are awake, we are not really fully awake but half-asleep or half-conscious. To awaken fully, the Guru's help is necessary.

Even when rain falls on top of the mountain, it will flow down. Such is the nature of the mind, too. We might momentarily feel that the mind is in an elevated realm but it will start sinking within seconds. No matter how many scriptures we study, the mind will, unbeknown to us, become attached to some sense object or other. The Guru knows well both the weaknesses of the mind and the means to overcome them. The nature of water is to flow down. But the same water will rise up as water vapor when it evaporates. Similarly, the Guru knows that, by kindling awareness in the disciple, he can uplift the disciple's mind to great heights. The Guru's aim is to kindle awareness in the disciple, and he strives tirelessly to do so. Once awareness is kindled, i.e. when the inner Guru has been awakened, the disciple will no longer need the outer Guru.

Every word of one whose awareness is illumined is a satsaṅg. His every act is a prayer and meditation. Every breath of such a person will benefit the world.

74. Smile Always, even during a Crisis

Children, we must be able to face every crisis in life with a smile. Whether we laugh or cry, life will continue. That being the case, is it not better to live with a smile? A smile is music of the soul.

Like every other decision, happiness is also a decision. If we resolve to be happy, no matter what, we can definitely create an atmosphere of joy in our life. The very presence of someone who is always cheerful awakens joy in others.

Some people might ask, "How can someone smile while facing a sorrowful experience or a major setback in life?" Facing problems with a smile does not mean that we will never have to undergo sorrowful experiences. There will be sorrows and failures in life but they must never make us lose our courage, presence of mind, and optimistic faith. Even if we lose these qualities, we must be able to regain them quickly. Many people start brooding, blaming others and despairing over minor setbacks. But there are also people who move ahead courageously and optimistically even in the face of intense sorrow. This is what is meant by smiling even during crises.

Some celebrate even disasters as if they were festivals. Lord Kṛṣṇa was well-known for his smile, which never faded from his face. In some countries, the bodies of the dead are taken to the graveyard in a procession marked by song and dance. They thus transform even death into a celebration.

Some people argue that those who have scaled the peaks of spirituality might be able to live life with a constant smile, but that it is not practical for ordinary people to face both joy and sorrow equally with a smile. Smiling during a crisis does not mean suppressing sorrow but not caving in under any circumstance. This is surmounting, not suppressing. There is nothing wrong with expressing grief when we are sad but we must not remain stuck in that state. We should pick ourselves up and move on.

A smile is not just the stretching of the facial muscles. Any act that benefits oneself and society is indeed a smile. Even if a person who does good deeds does not wear an outer smile, his kind heart itself is one big smile. In reality, there is a smile in each one of our good actions and loving words. A smile arising from a kind heart is consoling and inspiring. It is a medicine that heals all wounds.

75. Spirituality

Children, spirituality is knowledge of oneself. It is the realization of one's true nature. There is no use being a king if he does not know that he is a king. Even if there are priceless gems underneath a beggar's hut, he will remain a beggar for as long as he does not know about the treasure. Most of us are in a similar situation. People hurt each other for the sake of wealth and sensual pleasures. They also destroy nature. In order to uplift such people, we must go down to their level.

Once, a strangely dressed sorcerer came to a village. The villagers started making fun of him. When the ridiculing increased, the sorcerer became angry. He muttered some mantras into a handful of ash, which he dropped into the village well. He cursed everyone who drank from the well to become mad. Upon drinking the well water, all the villagers became mad. Only the village head remained sane, as he only drank water from his own well. All the other villagers started shouting whatever came to mind, dancing and raising a ruckus. When they noticed that the village head was not behaving like them, they were amazed. His behavior was so different from theirs that they concluded he was mad! They tried to catch him and tie him up. The scene was one of total chaos! He somehow managed to escape from their clutches. He thought, "All the villagers are mad. If I behave differently, they will not leave me alone. If I am to continue living here to uplift them, I've no other choice: I must behave like them. To catch a thief, one must dress like one." The village chief started to shout and dance like the others. The villagers were relieved to see that their chief had become normal.

The village head had another well dug and encouraged the villagers to drink water from the new well. Slowly, they became sane again.

Mahātmās (spiritually illumined souls) are like the village head in this story. Though they serve people without any expectation, people might ridicule them and even label them lunatics. Not that they are bothered by such challenges, as they regard praise and abuse equally. They go down to the level of people and, through their example, teach them to serve without expectation and to love without desire.

Spirituality is not just believing in God or performing religious rites. If religion is to become a bridge connecting human hearts instead of creating barriers between people, we must go beyond outer customs and observances to assimilate the essence of spirituality. Only then will *dharma* (righteousness), noble values and the attitude of selfless service prevail in society.

76. Responsibilities of the Media

Children, newspapers and television are now an indispensable part of life. We can even say that the media connects humanity the world over. They are mirrors of our country and the world. More than that, they are a beacon for society. The media shape public opinion. Therefore, they have a great responsibility towards society.

The media must become a means for refining the public mind. The increasing violence, injustice, corruption, conflict and other problems in society are all our own creation. Every problem first begins in the mind. For this very reason, our first duty is to refine the mind.

Samskāra encompasses goodness, noble values, uplifting customs, and the awareness of what is right. The media's duty is to unveil the truth and highlight wrongdoing. They must teach the public to distinguish between right and wrong. Today, most newspapers and other media do not maintain neutrality while presenting news and other programs but are aligned to one side or the other. This is far from ideal. The media ought to promote *dharma* (righteousness) and samskāra. They must rouse a slumbering society and inculcate discernment and samskāra in people.

Instead of giving undue coverage to negative tendencies and thus creating confusion, the media must highlight the noble and exemplary aspects of society. Instead of lulling people into a state of lethargy, the news and entertainment sections must guide them to the eternal music of wakefulness.

India and her soil have a unique scent: the eternal fragrance of values such as renunciation, love, austerity and spirituality. The loving bond between parents and children, the reverence that people have towards Gurus, and healthy relationships with neighbors—these constitute our wealth. Even our art forms were modes of worship. What we need is entertainment and knowledge that recognize this glorious heritage and culture. Only then can we mold an exemplary society. Blind imitation of the West will only sap us of our energy.

Bhārat's (India's) life motto is *Satyam, Śivam, Sundaram*—Truth, Auspiciousness, Beauty. The fundamental responsibility of the media is to find and interpret beauty in human life and nature. Only that which is true and auspicious can lead us to real beauty. Our focus should not only be on what is popular but also on what is good and beneficial to society.

May the media be able to impart knowledge and entertainment that is rooted in dharma and samskāra, and be the engine driving societal transformation.

77. Accept Everything as God's Gift

Children, it is natural for people to blame circumstances when they encounter failures in life. All of us blame other people or circumstances for our failures, sorrows and hardship. But if we reflect on this, we will realize that the fundamental reason for all our problems lies within ourselves. If we are prepared to turn within and recognize our weaknesses, we will be able to overcome any situation.

Suppose someone throws garbage from the upper floor of a house as we were walking by and it falls on us. We might feel angry with the person for tossing the waste out so carelessly. But if we see that he did not mean to throw it on us, we can also forgive him.

That said, there might be occasions when we will have no choice but to accept certain situations calmly, even when they are unfavorable. For example, imagine that a rotten mango falls on our head while we are strolling through a mango orchard, causing its putrid juices to drip down our forehead and cheeks. Suppose we angrily curse the mango and the mango tree, and then, further inflamed, curse the earth's gravitational pull also. We would be acting like a complete idiot because it is natural for ripe mangoes to fall from branches. We must learn to accept such situations without reacting in any way.

We can arrive at solutions to most problems in life through our own efforts. When others do wrong, we can either react against it or forgive them; we have the freedom to do one or the other. But there will be certain situations that we will have to accept as God's will or consider to be an inevitable part of life.

When faced with failures and problems, we must not blame circumstances or other people. Instead, we must learn to overcome our own weaknesses. We must find the real reasons for our failures and problems. We must not despair if we fail but redouble our efforts. If the situation is beyond our control, we must accept it instead of becoming distressed. In any circumstance, we must safeguard our presence of mind as if it were an invaluable gem.

When we receive *prasād*[14] from the temple, we might find small stones in it. We will remove them and eat the prasād with devotion. Similarly, we must be able to accept any situation with *prasāda-buddhi*, the attitude that it is a gift from God. Such an attitude will enhance our self-control and mental purity. We will also be able to maintain our cheerfulness.

[14] Offering to God, typically food, that is later shared among devotees as a consecrated gift.

78. Fear

Children, we are always gripped by fear of something or the other, and this is killing us every minute. Fear haunts us whether we are awake or sleeping. We are afraid to either do or not do anything.

Fear grips us when we feel that we cannot resolve problems. We magnify the problems that we are facing today and the ones we might face tomorrow, and then we start to worry. But if we bravely take one step forward, we will see our problems becoming more manageable. We are mostly worried about the future. But if we turn to look at the past, we will see that most of our fears were unfounded.

We need to be grounded in reality. Once we understand the nature of every object, we need not fear it. Fire is needed to cook food, to stave off the cold, to dispel darkness and for many other things. But if we touch fire, our hand will get burnt. So, if we understand its nature and how to use it properly, we need not fear fire. Similarly, the scriptures tell us to live with an understanding of the world. If we have a spiritual outlook on life, we will not succumb to fear needlessly.

We cannot completely renounce all our needs and desires, but we must curb our desires. If we do not do so, fear will never leave us. A man took a loan with interest to build a house, but was unable to repay the loan. The interest accumulated to such an extent that even if he sold the house, he would not be able to repay his debt. If he had prudently thought about how to repay the loan before taking it, he could have avoided this predicament. Therefore, we must distinguish between needs and luxuries.

Overwhelming fear does more harm than good. Fear can petrify the mind and hinder our ability to act. Two children were swimming in a pool. The mother of one child was with them. They were at the shallow end of the pool where the water was only two feet deep. The children were four feet tall, and so there was no question of them drowning there. Even so, within two minutes of their entering the pool, one of the boys started drowning and began to cry for help. Seeing this, the mother of the other boy lifted him up and said, "Look, your friend is swimming fearlessly. Why did you panic?"

The child said, "I became frightened when I thought that no one would rescue me if I started drowning. My legs became wobbly and I began to feel dizzy. Then I collapsed."

The woman asked her son, "Why is it that you had no fear?"

"You were nearby. I knew that if I started drowning, you would lift me out of the water. So, I had no fear," replied the son.

Faith in his mother gave the boy self-confidence, and awoke his innate abilities. Swimming became a joyful experience for him.

The benefit of having faith in God is similar. We must trust that the Almighty is always watching over us and will come to our rescue if any danger befalls us. That faith will give us the strength to face life courageously. When faith and discernment come together, fear will disappear.

79. Fear and Love

Children, fear is the main obstacle standing in the way of our attaining success in life. Fear robs us of our ability to harness our strengths and talents for our benefit. But there is a special power within that can help us overcome fear: love. Love gives us the strength to push aside every obstacle and move forward.

There was a widow living in a village. She made her living selling milk inside the king's fortress. One day, she climbed up as usual to the mountaintop fortress to sell milk. By the time she finished selling the milk, the fortress gates had closed. She tearfully pleaded with the guards, "My child is all alone in the hut. It's getting dark. If I don't reach home soon, my child will start crying in fear. If something happens to my child, I won't be able to survive. Please have mercy on me and allow me to leave the fortress."

But the guards were not willing to open the fortress gates. With utmost anguish, the milkmaid started searching for some other way out of the fortress.

When the fortress gates opened the next morning, the milkmaid was standing outside, waiting to enter. The guards were stunned. They could not understand how she had left the fortress. They took the woman to the king.

The king asked the milkmaid how she had left the fortress. The woman explained in detail what had happened. The king went with her to see the place from which she had exited the fortress. There was a small opening in the fortress wall. Even in the clear light of day, the climb down the sheer cliff face seemed impossible. The king asked the milkmaid, "While climbing down the mountain in the dark, didn't you feel even a little fear?"

The milkmaid said, "Yesterday, I had only one thought in mind: to reach my child somehow. I knew that my child would be frightened, not seeing me. I forgot myself. There was no place for fear in my heart."

Neither danger nor obstacles deterred the milkmaid. Her love for her child gave her the strength to overcome all problems.

When love fills our heart, if we are able to cherish a noble ideal or lofty goal, no obstacle can deter us. Even the fear of death will not daunt us. Love will give us the strength to face any danger.

80. Karma-yōga

Children, everyone in the world is usually steeped in action. Each one acts with the expectation of being benefited by the action. If we get what we desire, we become happy. If we do not, we become sad. When our expectation of a particular outcome becomes excessive, we lose our peace of mind. Anxiety over the outcome of an action makes the mind restless both while engaged in the action and afterwards. *Karma-yōga* is the means of transforming *karma* (action), which is the cause of bondage, into karma-yōga, which leads to Self-realization.

At times, we may not gain what we had hoped for, even though we worked hard. Suppose a farmer worked hard in the field. But when it was time for the harvest, heavy rains destroyed all the crops. From this, we can understand that the result of our actions does not depend only on our efforts. That is why in the *Bhagavad-Gītā*, Lord Kṛṣṇa gives so much importance to *niṣkāma karma,* i.e. selfless action.

Unless one is free from attachment, one can never succeed in the field of action. Often, our attachment to certain individuals and objects hinders the proper discharge of our duties. We can see many examples of this around us. The most experienced surgeon will not have the courage to operate on his own wife or child. A fair-minded judge might hesitate to pass judgment on his son, the prime accused in a murder case. From these examples, we can see the extent to which our attachment to people affects our efficiency.

Actually, it is not karma that binds but our pride in the karma and the desire for the fruits of action. Karma-yōga is the means by which one can do work with utmost efficiency and, at the same time, not be bound by action.

Amma remembers a story. Once, a man ate too much ghee (clarified butter) during a feast. The next day, he started suffering from indigestion. Unable to bear the stomachache, he went to see a doctor, who told him, "Bring me a liter of ghee. I shall prepare medicine with it".

The man was taken aback. He said, "Doctor, I'm suffering from indigestion because I ate too much ghee. Do you want to aggravate my condition by making me take even more ghee?"

But the doctor insisted, and the patient reluctantly brought a liter of ghee. The doctor added some herbs to it and dispensed titrated dosages to the patient. The man recovered.

In the same way, actions performed carelessly or with the wrong attitude make life miserable. But the solution is also action, albeit action done without ego and attachment. Karma is not dangerous if the attitude behind it is correct. It will benefit the world.

The karma yōgī knows that the result of action is not in his hands and that he is merely an instrument in God's hands. Therefore, he performs every action, no matter what, with utmost sincerity, and accepts the outcome, whatever it is, as God's will. He does not become anxious about the fruits of his action.

Karma-yōga is the most practical way of working. It is the path leading to the ultimate goal of spiritual liberation. May my children have the strength to advance on this path.

81. Youth and Intoxicants

Children, addiction to intoxicants is one of the biggest pitfalls that the youth of today face. Parents send their children to schools in the hope that they will make it big in life. But the children may fall into bad company and become enslaved by bad habits. Instead of becoming a support and solace to their parents and a pride to the nation, young people destroy themselves and harm others.

The idea that drugs can give one happiness is a myth. Trying to find happiness in external objects is like trying to stoke a fire by blowing on a firefly!

In a village, there lived a boy who used to study hard. He had no bad habits and never spent money unnecessarily. If his parents gave him pocket money, he would give the money to poor students so that they could pay their school fees, or he would buy textbooks or school uniforms for them. He was admired by all.

One day, a few classmates forcibly took him to a cinema. On the way back, they started smoking and offered him a cigarette. When he declined, they asked him to try smoking just once. After he had smoked one cigarette, they encouraged him to try smoking again. He thought that there was nothing wrong with smoking one or two cigarettes.

On another occasion, at their insistence, he drank some beer. Soon, smoking, drinking and taking drugs became habitual. He started demanding money from his parents to pay for these habits. The very boy who used to touch his parents' feet reverentially every morning before going to school lost all respect for them. He began fighting with them daily for money. But no matter how much money he received, it was never enough. Eventually, he started stealing and extorting money.

Once, when he was high on drugs, he attacked a man, who died as a result. The boy was convicted and sent to prison. This boy had once been the darling of the villagers, his teachers and his classmates. But when he became a thief, thug and menace to society, they detested him.

Friendship is like an elevator; it can take us up or down, depending on which button we press. Likewise, good company helps us progress towards a bright future whereas bad company leads to our downfall and destruction. When we see a stagnant puddle on our path, we carefully avoid it. Similarly, if wayward people try to become our friends, we must wisely steer clear of them.

82. Corruption

Children, the number of religious people in our country is increasing. Places of worship are swelling with more and more people. Yet, corruption and a deterioration of values are becoming rampant in society. Incidents involving the sexual harassment of women and acts of violence are on the rise. Some people ask how we can explain this contradiction.

There is corruption in one form or another, not just in India, but all over the world. It is just a question of degree. People believe in God but their knowledge of spiritual principles is limited. Their religious awareness is confined to praying for the fulfilment of desire and to celebrating religious rituals and festivals. The prevailing view—that the goal of life is to make as much money as possible so as to enjoy material comforts—has gained in strength today. So, even though the numbers of believers have increased, we cannot see a corresponding increase in the benefits of devotion in society. Yet, we cannot say that believing in God has not brought about any change in society either. It is because of faith that *dharma* (righteousness) prevails in the world to the extent that it does.

There is no point in lamenting over how degraded society has become. Before blaming others, we must first examine ourselves. We must turn within, realize our own defects, and sincerely try to correct them.

There was a poor farmer who used to sell butter to the proprietor of a bakery nearby. After some time, the baker began to suspect that the farmer was giving him less butter than before. He started weighing the butter and saw that there was a significant difference. He filed a case against the poor farmer, alleging that the farmer had been cheating him. The poor farmer was summoned to court, where the judge ordered the farmer's weighing scales to be brought before him. The farmer earnestly said, "Sir, I don't have a weighing scale or any weights. I buy bread from his bakery. I used to give him as much butter as the bread weighed. If the quantity of butter is less than it used to be, then the baker is responsible for it."

We need not wait for others to improve before trying to reform ourselves. We must change first. Each one of us must become a role model to others because, knowingly or unknowingly, someone is following our example.

Good and evil start at home. Parents must become role models for their children. Homes and schools must create an environment that is conducive to the inculcation of values. We can then eliminate, to some extent at least, the corruption that exists in all spheres of life. In this way, at least future generations can be freed from the clutches of corruption.

83. Youth

Children, youth is the most dynamic period in human life. Young people have energy and enthusiasm. They long to engage in activity and to accomplish great things. Youth is usually also the time when one is imbued with idealism. The only problem is that the lively and impulsive actions of youngsters sometimes reveal a lack of patience and maturity. Young people have knowledge but lack awareness. For as long as we lack discernment, our knowledge will be imperfect, like a flower without fragrance or a word without meaning. Real transformation occurs when knowledge and awareness unite.

If young people are given proper knowledge and direction and if their energies are harnessed properly, society can achieve great things through them. Swāmī Vivēkānanda was a great personality who understood the potential of youth and who strove to channel their strengths in the right direction. It is not surprising that his blend of wisdom, courage, idealism and zealous desire to do good to society made him a role model for young people.

Laziness, a lack of self-confidence, and the fear of failure are what holds us back. We can conquer these with an indomitable will, right knowledge and untiring efforts. Young people must realize that old age awaits them in the not too distant future. They must do whatever is necessary to fulfil their lives while they are young and healthy.

Youngsters have vigor and vitality. If their energy can be channeled in the right direction, they can create wonders in this world. If the young change, the world will change. If we wish to harness the power of youth to transform society, we must first foster *lakṣya-bōdha* (goal-orientedness) in them. Their goals should not be confined just to finding a good job and leading a comfortable life. It is not enough to catch fish from the surface of the ocean. We must dive deep into life in order to collect precious pearls.

Youth must be able to transform society creatively and to find fulfilment in their own lives. They must have both material knowledge and a spiritual outlook. Their hearts must empathize with the suffering people around them. They must gain the spiritual strength to face the challenges of life boldly and to forge ahead without losing heart. Great achievements are possible only through sacrifice. Therefore, they must be prepared to undergo difficulties and sacrifices. They must gain the courage to recognize and assimilate goodness wherever they see it and to turn away from evil.

The culture of our country can help us achieve all this. She has given birth to many ideal role models like Vivēkānanda. Our sages imparted the knowledge that helps one overcome all sorrow. It is enough to direct the attention of our youth to this invaluable wealth.

When knowledge and discernment converge, all of one's inner capabilities will be enhanced, and one will be able to find love, peace, happiness and success in life.

84. Be Grateful

Children, gratitude is one of the noble qualities every human being must have. Behind every one of our victories are the encouragement, help and guidance of many people. We must be grateful to all of them. As it is God's grace that brings any effort to fruition, we must be grateful to God as well. We can also learn many lessons from the bitter experiences of life. They help us become purer and stronger. So, we ought to be grateful to life itself.

Once, a beggar found a bag of old gold coins lying by the wayside. He went to the palace and gave the bag to the king, who realized, to his delight, that these were the precious coins he had lost years ago. Pleased with the beggar's honesty, the king appointed him minister in charge of the royal treasury. The other ministers did not like this at all.

After a few days, they reported to the king that many items were disappearing from the treasury and alleged that the new minister was behind the disappearance. Every day, the new minister would arrive at and leave the palace with a bundle in hand. The other ministers said that the bundle contained items stolen from the treasury and that the new minister was taking this stash home. The king found this hard to believe and decided to verify the matter for himself.

The next day, he hid in the treasury's loft. As usual, the minister reached the treasury. He opened the bundle and took out some old rags. These were the clothes he used to wear when he was a beggar. He changed into the tattered robes of the beggar, stood in front of a mirror, and said to himself, "By God's grace, you have become a minister. Always be grateful for this. You may lose all this power and prestige tomorrow. Change is the nature of the world. Welcome all the experiences that life gives you. Be grateful to life."

Touched by his words, the king climbed down at once and embraced the minister lovingly. As there was no heir to the throne, the king declared the minister his successor.

Like the minister in the story, we must always have a heart filled with gratitude. We must not become arrogant over our victories, small or big. We must always be grateful to those who guided us, to the circumstances that led to our success, and, above all, to God. Contentment and gratitude ought to be the hallmarks of our life.

85. Science and Spirituality

Children, both science and spirituality are striving to discover the truth behind the universe—science, through external enquiry, and spirituality, through an inner search. Science sees the object of investigation as separate from the investigator. We perceive this world through the sense organs, mind and intellect. We can never gain knowledge of any object without recourse to the sense organs, mind and intellect.

An ant does not see an elephant in the same way as a human being does. Its eyesight is different from ours, and therefore, it can never see the real shape of an elephant. Similarly, a cockroach will see an elephant in yet another way. From this, we can see that our impression of the universe is dependent on our limited sense organs, mind and intellect. It is not an accurate picture.

The universe around us is in a constant state of flux. A seed that is planted in the soil grows into a tree. Eventually, that tree also dies. A pot is made of clay. When the pot is destroyed, it is reduced to clay again. In truth, nothing is destroyed, only the attributes keep changing. Amidst all this change, there is something that remains unchanged—the substratum of pure consciousness, which is devoid of attributes.

The discoveries and theories of science are predicated on the limited knowledge of the times. Therefore, the postulates of today might be proven wrong tomorrow. Today, we might discover a new drug. After some time, we might find out about its adverse side effects. By the time it is recalled from stores, quite a few people might have almost died as a result of taking that medicine.

In this sense, the history of science is a continuing saga of trial, error and new discoveries. No matter how many discoveries science makes, there will always remain much more to be discovered. It is like two lawyers arguing in the absence of a judge; their argument will never end. In the quest to discover the truth of the universe, spirituality plays the role of judge. In spirituality, there is a successful ending. The substratum of the universe is consciousness, and one is nothing but that. When one realizes that the universe is a manifestation of that consciousness, the search for Truth comes to an end.

86. See God in Everything

Children, many people wonder if the Indian customs and traditions of worship are primitive. At first glance, they may seem so, but if we understand and assimilate the principles and ideals behind the practices, we will see that they are actually meaningful and beneficial. Otherwise, they will be nothing more than empty rituals.

Divine consciousness enlivens everything in nature. God is the essence of all beings, both moving and unmoving. Nature is a manifestation of God. The ancient sages realized the Truth and beheld divine consciousness in everything. Thus, the worship of birds, beasts, trees, mountains, rivers and forests became part of our culture. There is nothing in the universe that is not worthy of worship, for God dwells in everything. Worshipping everything as a manifestation of God without distinguishing between low or high is an easy way to realize the all-pervading nature of God.

If God is perfect and complete, then his creation is also perfect and complete. If we use the flame from a lamp to kindle a thousand other lamps, these lamps will burn just as brightly as the first lamp. Is there any lamp that we can single out for being imperfect or incomplete? In this universe, which God pervades, there is nothing we can consider base or ignoble. That said, we need eyes that can perceive this perfection.

Every creature in nature is interconnected. When all creatures coexist harmoniously, life becomes joyful. Man survives only because of flora and fauna. Without them, there can be no humankind or human culture. All other creatures uphold the balance in nature; man alone disturbs it. Because of his selfishness and excessive desire for pleasure, he hurts everything in nature and even kills his fellow men. Man is the only false note in the harmonious melody of nature.

Our ancestors understood how every creature played a significant role in maintaining the balance in the environment. That is why they designed practical methods to protect birds, snakes, trees and groves. The traditions and rituals that they bequeathed were also meant to maintain the balance of nature. None of these practices pollute nature. Thus, they created a culture that regards nature as Mother and protects Her. It taught us to love and serve everyone.

Actually, what is wrong with worshipping animals? In many ways, they are more evolved than mankind. Many animals have a much more powerful sense of sight, hearing and smell. Birds and beasts sense natural disasters before humans do and move to safer places. Man can learn the lessons of unity and enthusiasm from ants. How else can we look upon creatures, trees, mountains and forests, which make life conducive for us, other than with respect and reverence?

Our ancestors used to touch the earth reverentially as soon as they woke up. We must learn to bow down to any object we use. Our hearts will become expansive if we can see all creatures as manifestations of God. We will feel love towards all. We will be able to open our hearts to flora and fauna. We will gain the attitude of bowing down before even an ant. We will be able to experience divine consciousness in everything. The greatest spiritual practice is seeing God in everything. It is also the ultimate realization.

87. Vasudhaiva Kuṭumbakam —the World is One Family

Children, the survival of the world hinges on love and compassion. Even though there are many waves of anger, hatred and selfishness in the world today, there are also surges of love, compassion and selflessness arising in certain corners. It is the vibrations of compassion that maintain the balance of the world.

Many species of birds and beasts are on the brink of extinction. Though this is a serious issue, we are not aware of a much graver problem: the near extinction of compassionate people. While it is true that such people have not become extinct yet, kind hearts are fast disappearing from the world. We must wake up to and think about the consequences. Many of us take pride in the intellectual strides we have made but we are not aware that the heart has dried up.

Once, students in a school for the mentally challenged were performing a play on stage. There was a scene in which a beggar seeks shelter from the freezing cold for the night. When he goes to a mansion, the people living there scold him and drive him away. Feeling hurt, he leaves. Seeing this, one of the mentally challenged students in the audience was moved. He went up to the stage and said, "Don't be sad. Come home with me. There is space in my room for another person." Hearing these innocent words, the audience started applauding in appreciation. Many eyes welled up with tears. How many of us, who pride ourselves on our intelligence, have as much compassion as this mentally challenged child?

Today, society has become trapped in the cycle of selfishness and greed. Love and compassion are not meant to be confined to family and friends. Love is seeing oneself in others. When the 'I' sense disappears completely, love becomes compassion. When we think, "my home" or "my people," others are excluded. On the contrary, if we think of ourselves as one, as beads strung on the thread of life, everyone becomes 'our own.'

When love overflows towards all the beings in the universe, the whole world becomes one family. This is what our ancestors meant when they said "*vasudhaiva kuṭumbakam.*"

88. Universal Peace

Children, in general, people today are discontented and perturbed. Human minds are filled with fear and suspicion. Given a chance, people and nations will trample down and destroy each other. Selfishness and egoism have turned life into a battlefield. Such is the world we live in.

This does not mean that goodness has disappeared completely from the world. There are many people working ceaselessly for the benefit of humanity. Nevertheless, the degree of evil is worsening, and goodness is not flourishing sufficiently to check the burgeoning of evil.

A rich man met his friend after many years. He told his old friend, "Let's go and sit down for a while in the park nearby." On the way there, the rich man said, "We played together and grew up together. We also studied in the same school. But there's a world of difference between us now."

His friend did not say anything. After some time, the rich man suddenly stopped. He picked up a five-rupee coin from the ground and said, "This fell from your pocket." They continued walking. Suddenly, the friend stopped and went to a thorny bush nearby. A butterfly trapped between thorns was flapping its wings frantically. The friend slowly and carefully freed the butterfly from the thorns and watched as it fluttered happily into the sky. Seeing this, the rich man asked, "How did the butterfly catch your attention?"

His friend replied, "Like you said, there's a huge difference between us. It is this: you hear the clink of coins whereas I hear the heartbeat."

Look at the difference between their attitudes. Our thoughts and actions determine our *samskāra* (disposition) and personality. Everyone should be made aware from childhood itself of the goodness that arises from love and co-operation and of the disasters wrought by hatred and conflict.

We must strive to understand the feelings of others and act accordingly. Each nation must become the eyes, ears, voice, heart, mind and body of other nations. Only then can they understand the sorrows and difficulties of other countries and respond appropriately. Only then can the world grow as one single entity. Only through such growth can we have equality, kinship and peace.

Path to Peace

Children, Amma feels sad when she looks at the world today. We can see pictures of bloodshed and tears everywhere. We do not show mercy even to small children. How many innocent people are dying daily because of wars and terrorist attacks in various parts of the world? There were wars in the past, too. But in those days, people used to comply with war conventions such as not attacking the unarmed and not fighting after sunset. But today, any atrocity or unrighteous act is considered acceptable. Selfishness and egoism rule the world.

The root cause of all destruction is the ego. The worst destruction is wreaked by two types of egos: one, the ego of power and money; two, the ego that says, "Only my vision is true. I will not tolerate any other viewpoint." Unless we become free of such egos, we cannot enjoy peace in life.

All viewpoints are important. We must respect everyone's viewpoint and try to take it into consideration. If we do so, we can stop these senseless wars and bloodshed.

In order to understand and respect the viewpoints of others, we must awaken the love within us. Many of us show great interest in learning new languages. But no language other than that of love can help us truly understand each other. We have completely forgotten this language.

Amma remembers an incident. Once, volunteers of a humanitarian organization went to see a wealthy businessman to solicit funds for their humanitarian activities. They spoke at length about the sad plight of those who were suffering. Their description would have melted anyone's heart but the businessman was not interested in listening to them. As the disappointed volunteers got up to leave, the businessman said, "Wait. Let me ask you a question. If you can give the correct answer, I'll help you. I have an artificial eye. Can you tell me which one it is?"

They looked carefully at his eyes. One of them said, "The left eye is artificial."

"Amazing! So far, no one has ever been able to detect the artificial eye, which is very expensive. How did you detect it?"

The social worker said, "I gazed deeply into both your eyes. I saw a trace of compassion in your left eye whereas your right eye was as hard as stone. That's why I was sure that your real eye is the right one!"

This *businessman* is the symbol of our times. Our heads are heated by egoism, and our hearts are frozen by selfishness. It should be otherwise. The heart should be warm with love and compassion. The head should be cool with the expansiveness of wisdom.

Love and compassion are our greatest wealth, but we have lost that wealth. Neither we nor the world can survive unless we restore the tenderness of love to our eyes. We must awaken that tenderness within.

Peace and Contentment

Children, many organizations and individuals are working tirelessly for world peace and happiness. Notwithstanding that, goodness has not been strong enough to resist the proliferation of evil. We have forgotten the love, respect and trust that human beings ought to show one another. Everyone thinks only of fulfilling his or her own desires at any cost.

We spend millions on national security and fighting wars, sacrificing countless lives for this. If we allocate even a tiny portion of this money and human effort to promote world peace instead, we will definitely be able to maintain peace and harmony.

We have forgotten the fundamental truth that the human mind is the cause of all the problems in the world and that the world will improve only if the mind improves. Religion and spirituality help to transform anger into compassion, hatred into love, and jealousy into sympathy. A society is made up of individuals. It is the conflict in the human mind that leads to war. When change takes place in the individual, society will automatically change. Instead of brooding revenge and hatred, let us foster love and peace in the mind. All we need to do is try.

It is not the times that create change but compassionate hearts. We must be able to nurture more such hearts. This ought to be our foremost aim.

Let us try to cultivate a heart that can forgive and forget, thus giving the world a new lease of life. There is no point in excavating the past. It will not benefit the world or its people. Abandoning the path of enmity and revenge, we must impartially assess the current state of affairs in the world. Only then can we find the path to progress.

This is the age of unity. We will achieve our goals only if we work together. What the world needs today are people who are noble in word and deed. If there are such role models who can inspire their fellow beings, the darkness shrouding society will be dispelled by the light of peace and harmony. Let us work together to achieve this.

May the tree of life be rooted firmly in the soil of love. May good deeds be its leaves, kind words its flowers, and peace its fruit. May the world become one family, united in love. May we become the proud owners of a world illumined by peace and contentment.

The World is a Flower

Today, the world today is like a hornbill 15 thirsting for the clear rainwater of love and peace. Clashes, terrorist attacks and wars are taking place every day in one place or another. Even now, countless lives are being sacrificed.

In order to stop this senseless human sacrifice, we must first understand its causes. To foil terrorist attacks, security measures have been put into place in airports and other places. Stringent safety checks have become mandatory. This is all very good. But they can never be permanent solutions. There is another explosive device even more lethal than a bomb. It can never be detected by any machine. It is the hatred, hostility and enmity in human minds.

Amma remembers a story. A village head was celebrating his hundredth birthday. A journalist asked him, "In your hundred years, what achievement are you proudest of?"

He said, "Though I have lived a hundred years, I don't have even a single enemy!"

[15] According to Indian mythology, the hornbill drinks only raindrops and does not relish any other water.

"How wonderful!" exclaimed the journalist. "Everyone should follow your example. Tell us, how was this possible?"

The village head replied, "Oh! I never let any of my enemies stay alive!"

This is how many in the world rid themselves of enemies. But there is another way to destroy the enemy: by transforming a foe into a friend, by opening up our heart and expressing love towards the enemy. There will definitely be a change of heart in the enemy. Without such patience and love, it will be difficult to bring about peace and harmony in society.

Hatred, rivalry and conflict are the nature of the world. Some might argue that it is not possible to change this. This is not true. The basic nature of man is love and goodness. Therefore, if we try, we can replace these emotions with love and compassion.

We must light the lamp of hope and consolation in the hearts of the victims of war and conflict. We must be ready to love with our hearts and serve with our hands. When we are ready to open our own hearts to understand others and share their sorrows, our own weaknesses will fall away, one by one. Gradually, we and society will improve and grow.

Imagine that a dear friend whom you have not seen for a long time is going to visit you. You will be jumping for joy. You will make all the necessary preparations to receive him. You will clean and decorate the house, cook a sumptuous meal, and wait enthusiastically for him. We ought to be able to welcome every moment of life with this attitude. Let us spend every moment serving others joyfully and enthusiastically, and thus make every moment as beneficial as possible.

When the goodness within awakens, society will awaken. Peace and contentment will prevail. We will be able to see the whole world as a flower and everyone in the world as different petals of that flower, undivided by the boundaries of nation and language. We will behold beauty everywhere, and see unity in diversity. The whole world will become one family.

89. Devotion and Life

Children, many of us remember God only when faced with problems. Our devotion is limited; we pray and make offerings to God so that He will solve our problems and fulfil our desires. At other times, we forget God completely. We cannot call this devotion. True devotion is not a part-time affair. A devotee remembers God in all circumstances.

Some people were waiting outside a shop to buy things. The shopkeeper was busy wrapping their purchases. Suddenly, he stopped working, closed his eyes, and stood there with joined palms. After a while, when he opened his eyes, one of his customers angrily asked, "What injustice is this? Is it right of you to stand there with eyes closed when so many of us are waiting?"

The shopkeeper calmly replied, "Didn't you hear the *dīpārādhana*[16] bells from the nearby temple? As soon as I heard the ringing, I closed my eyes for a while to pray."

The people gathered in front of the shop said, "We didn't hear any bell ringing from the temple."

Hearing this, the shopkeeper did not say anything and resumed his work. After a while, he took out a coin and threw it onto the street outside. No one noticed him throwing the coin but they all heard the clink of the coin as it fell to the ground and turned to look. A few of them even scrambled to pick it up. The shopkeeper said, "See, even when the temple bells clanged loudly,

[16] Waving lighted lamps, usually part of ceremonial worship.

none of you heard it, but the moment you heard the soft clink of the coin falling to the ground, your attention went towards it."

Those who came to buy things from the shop were focused on wealth and worldly objects. Therefore, they easily heard the sound of the coin. However, for the shopkeeper, God was the focal point in his life. Therefore, even while immersed in work, his attention was on God. When the person who is dearest to us has been hospitalized, our thoughts will revolve around him even while engaged in office work. Thoughts of him will continue flowing as an undercurrent amidst all our actions.

Likewise, God should become the center-point of our life. If so, no matter what we are doing and even if we are mired in worldly activities, our attention will be on God. We will be able to maintain a constant remembrance of God. This is true devotion.

90. True Knowledge

Children, three things are essential in life: knowledge, health and wealth. Many of us believe that if we are wealthy, we have everything. But what if we lose our health? We do not appreciate the value of health when we have it. Knowledge is even more important than the other two. Even if we have health and wealth but no knowledge, we will think and act indiscriminately, and this can ruin us.

Suppose we are the Prime Minister of a country. One careless word is all it might take for us to lose our position. An uprising might break out in the country, causing many thousands to lose their lives. Therefore, wisdom is of paramount importance. Even if we lose our health and wealth and life proves to be full of suffering, we can face every challenge cheerfully if we have true knowledge.

Once, there was a righteous king who loved and protected all his subjects like his own children. His virtues endeared him to his subjects, who revered him as if he were God. His fame spread in all directions. The neighboring kings became jealous, and they jointly conspired to destroy him. They bribed the king's minister, promised him position and power, and thus bought him. With his help, they launched a sudden and swift attack on the kingdom and captured the king. He was not given any special consideration but thrown into an ordinary jail with other prisoners. But even there, the king remained joyful, without any sign of distress. Seeing this, the enemy kings became disheartened and asked him, "Even though you have lost your power and wealth and are languishing in prison, you don't seem affected at all. Why?"

The king said, "You can defeat me in battle, imprison me, and torment me physically. But I am free to decide whether I want to be sad or happy. I have gained the highest knowledge, which makes even intense sorrow insignificant. I know who I am and I know the nature of the world. Knowing this, I have brought my mind completely under my control. You can do nothing to me."

We must first of all gain the knowledge of our true self and the nature of the world. Once we have gained this knowledge, we will be able to overcome any circumstance.

91. Śraddhā

Children, *śraddhā* (alertness) is an essential quality in any field of life. We must become aware of every thought, word and deed. We must also be aware of how we walk, sit and look.

Most of us spend all our time thinking of what is already over and of what is yet to come. Caught up in too many matters and problems, the mind is utterly scattered. As a result, we are unable to focus sufficiently on anything and succeed in it. In the mad rush to fulfil our desires, we do not do anything properly.

Amma remembers a story. Any patient occupying one particular bed in the ICU of a hospital would die on Sunday at around eleven a.m. The doctors were perplexed! Some even began to believe that an unearthly force was responsible for these deaths.

Finally, an expert committee was formed to look into this phenomenon. The next Sunday, a few minutes before eleven, doctors, experts, nurses and hospital authorities waited impatiently in the corridor outside the ICU where the deaths took place. A few held rosaries and were chanting. Others were praying.

At eleven sharp, a cleaner who worked only on Sundays entered the ICU, removed the plug connecting the patient to the life support system, and plugged in his vacuum cleaner. Thus, the mystery behind the Sunday deaths was solved.

Action done without alertness is *adharma* (unrighteous). It can bring us and others sorrow. There is no point in blaming God for our suffering. Doing so would be akin to driving carelessly, colliding into something, and then blaming the petrol for the accident.

The alertness that we demonstrate even in small matters helps us attain great things. One who is mindful of the goal will be alert in every thought, word and action.

We must always remain alert, like a soldier on a battlefield or a student in the examination hall. Training ourselves to do what needs to be done in every moment, with perfect attention, will transform that action into a great spiritual discipline. Work done with total awareness will take us swiftly to God. If we live 'today' with awareness, 'tomorrow' will become our friend.

92. Moral Consciousness

Children, righteous citizens lead a nation to prosperity. If we probe into the root cause of the problems besetting our country—corruption, poverty, unemployment, conflicts and increasing suicides, to name a few—we will see that it is the decline in moral awareness among people.

Following one's own dharma (*swadharma* or action suited to one's nature) is the duty of every individual. Rights and responsibilities are like the two wings of a bird. Only if both work in tandem can there be any real progress. If everyone in society discharges his or her duties properly, their rights will naturally be safeguarded. In contrast, if people are concerned only with their rights, the social order will be disrupted and lawlessness will prevail. Therefore, everyone must be prepared to work not only for personal needs but also for the welfare of society.

After every harvest, a farmer sets aside some seeds to be sown later. He knows that this is no loss as he will eventually get a yield that is a hundred times what he sowed. Instead, if he consumes the entire harvest, he will have to face poverty later. Similarly, we must also be ready to sacrifice. Instead of spending all our time and energy only for ourselves, we must be ready to spend at least a little time for the benefit of society and the country.

The Great Wall of China is one of the great wonders of the world. After it was built, the Chinese thought, "Now, no enemy will ever be able to defeat us." But before long, China was attacked. In a surprise move, the adversaries breached the Wall, entered the country, and swiftly overthrew the authorities. How did this happen? The guards at the Great Wall had accepted bribes from the enemy and let them in.

The pleasure we gain through selfish and unrighteous acts is fleeting. Such acts will undoubtedly become the cause of sorrow later. In contrast, even though selfless acts might seem onerous at first, they will bring about lasting goodness in due course. Let us not forget that the pleasure we gain as a result of unrighteous acts contains within it the seeds of sorrow.

In olden days, when children began their education, they were first taught about *dharma* (righteousness). Dharma is the principle of reciprocal nourishment governing the relationship between man and man and between man and nature. It is a healthy outlook on life and the universe. One cannot progress in life by one's own efforts alone. Our growth is dependent on the growth of others. Any lasting personal goodness can come about only through an improvement in the well-being of society.

93. Power of Youth

Children, consider the present situation of our country. How many problems bedevil us! Poverty, illiteracy, unemployment, social conflict, new diseases, increasing suicides, corruption, lethargy and aimlessness are just some of the problems we face.

We live in a society that is concerned only about itself. Such is our country today. Every faction of society thinks only about its own interests. Whether students, workers, politicians, religious groups, media, or the different states, all of them are intent only on protecting and promoting their own interests. No one is bothered about national interests or the common good.

All of us want to see a big change in society. Where should change begin? If we think, "Let others change first, let circumstances change, let the government do what is necessary, and then I will change," change will never happen. Change must start with us. If we change, we can bring about a change in those with whom we interact. Like waves rising in succession, change will gradually ripple throughout society and thus pave the way for a positive transformation in the country.

Amma remembers a story. There was a man who used to pray, "May my country improve. May people everywhere become truthful, enthusiastic and idealistic." But even after praying for years, he saw no change. When he realized that it was difficult to change the whole country, he started praying that at least his family members would set good examples for others. After many months, he realized that this prayer was also fruitless.

Finally, he started praying, "O God, please nurture noble qualities in me. May I be able to live with moral awareness and behave lovingly to everyone."

When he finished praying that day, he felt God whispering in his ears, "If you had been prepared to pray and strive like this earlier, how many positive changes would have taken place in this country by now!"

Young people are always the means through which a new society can be created. They naturally have enthusiasm and admiration for noble ideals. They also have high energy levels. If this energy is harnessed properly, young people can help to bring about a huge social transformation. All we need to do is inspire them. May they become like flowers spreading a sweet fragrance throughout the world.

94. Experience of God

Children, people have different ideas about God. Though some deny the existence of God, most people believe in him. Among believers, most consider God an external power, one that is separate from them. In reality, God dwells in all beings, both moving and unmoving, like the tree in a seed, butter in milk, and gold in gold ornaments.

There is divinity in every being. If we move along the right path, we can experience this inner divinity. Can one convey the taste of honey or the beauty of nature through words? It can be known only through experience. Similarly, the experience of God is far beyond the reach of words, sensory perception and the mind.

A *sanyāsī* (ordained monk) was passing a school. A few students asked him: "Why are you wearing these robes?"

The sanyāsī said, "I became a sanyāsī to realize God."

The children asked, "Has anyone seen God? How can one realize him?"

Pointing to a tree, the sanyāsī asked, "Where did this tree come from?"

"From the seed," answered the students. There were many fruits scattered under the tree. The sanyāsī picked up a fruit and bit into it. He looked inside and then threw it aside. He picked up another fruit, bit it, looked inside and threw it away. Seeing this, the students asked him, "What are you doing? Why are you biting these fruits and throwing them away?"

The sanyāsī replied "You said that this tree came from a seed. I was looking to see if the tree was inside the seed of the fruit."

Hearing this, the students laughed and said, "How can such a huge tree be inside such a tiny seed? You must first sow the seed, and then water and fertilize it regularly. After some time, it will sprout and grow into a huge tree over many years."

The sanyāsī said, "It is the same with God. Like the tree within the seed, God dwells in each one of you but you have yet to experience this. This does not mean that there is no God. If we follow the guidance of those who have realized God, anyone can experience Him."

God is an experience. The means to experiencing him include spiritual practices such as prayer, *japa* (repeated chanting of a mantra) and meditation. When a flower is still a bud, we will not be able to tell how fragrant or beautiful it will be. It must blossom. Likewise, the flower of our heart must blossom through meditation. Then we will be able to see God and experience supreme bliss.

95. Be a Witness

Children, even trivial incidents in the outer world can affect our mind. Some incidents make us happy whereas others make us sad. Some people wonder how one can remain poised between these two extremes, like a detached witness.

All of us have the capacity to step back and see everything as an observer. However, we rarely recognize this capacity or use it to our advantage. When other people face problems, we are detached and can even offer practical advice. But when we face the same problems, we crumble. This defeat is caused by the sense of 'I' and 'mine.'

Once, a disciple asked his Guru, "O Master, it's difficult to see everything with the attitude of a witness. How is it possible?"

The Guru did not answer. The disciple had made some careless mistakes, but the Guru said that another person had made all those mistakes. The disciple heard him out with a smile. Suddenly, the Guru said, "He didn't do any of those things. It was you who made all those mistakes!" Hearing this, the disciple's face turned pale and he hung his head in shame. The Guru then said, "When I pointed out your mistakes, you became sad. But when I blamed someone else earlier for those mistakes, you were able to receive it with the attitude of a witness. Therefore, you have the capacity to be a witness. When you realize that whatever you associate with 'I' now is not the real you, you will be able to summon the attitude of a witness. We have the capacity to observe our own thoughts and actions constantly. If you can cultivate this awareness further, you will be able to remain a witness in all circumstances and accept everything with a smile. Nothing will be able to affect your mental equilibrium."

While traveling in a bus, we might see many beautiful scenes—grand buildings and lovely gardens. We might also see unsettling sights. Nevertheless, we do not get flustered by them because we know that they are not our destination. We must be able to see the thoughts passing through the mind in the same way. See everything but remain detached from it all. This is what we need to cultivate.

96. Discontentment

Children, we often feel sad, thinking of the good fortune of others and of our own difficulties in life. We are constantly striving to be someone else. A woman wants to be a man. A man wants to be a woman. A child wants to be a grownup. The old long to become young. We are acutely conscious of all that we lack but do not appreciate the blessings God has given us.

A man prayed to God, "O Lord, my wife is not aware of my hardships. I work all day whereas she stays at home comfortably. I have a request: change me into her and change her into me."

Immediately, he heard the voice of God: "I shall grant you your prayers."

When he woke up the next day, he realized that he had become a woman. His wife, who had become a man, only needed to wake up at eight, bathe leisurely, and go to work, whereas he, who had become a woman, had to wake up early. He cooked breakfast, swept and cleaned the whole house, and bathed and fed the children. By then, it was time for the husband to go to work. After giving him his ironed clothes, she dropped the kids off at school. On the way back, she stopped at the market to buy vegetables. As soon as she got home, she did the laundry and then started preparing the evening meal. Suddenly, it started to rain. She ran out to bring in the clothes she had hung to dry and folded the dry ones. Soon, her husband and children returned home. She gave them tea and biscuits. She then lit the prayer lamp and sat down for prayers. She made the children do their homework. After serving her husband dinner, she started making the necessary preparations for the next day.

Days passed this way. By then, the husband-turned-wife had become exhausted. He prayed to God, "O Lord, wanting to become a woman was a big mistake! I'm exhausted. Please make me a man once again."

The Lord replied, "Okay, but you must wait nine months."

"Why, my Lord?"

"Because you're pregnant."

Each one of us is like the husband in the story. We are eager to compare ourselves to those who are better off and more capable. We do not realize that we are so much more fortunate than many people, who are in much worse situations.

Each one in the world is unique. Everyone occupies a singular place in the universe. Understanding this, we must awaken our potential and self-confidence and play our part in the world. Only then will we be content.

97. International Women's Day[17]

Children, a few days ago, a woman came to me with her two young children. Crying, she said, "Amma, my husband wastes all his earnings on alcohol. There are fights at home all the time. There is no peace at all. He even hits me and shouts at me in front of the children. I'm unable to look after my children properly. Amma, please save me!"

There are many such women in our country who are constantly shedding tears of sorrow. I am not saying that men do not suffer; some certainly do. But if we look at the world, we will see that 90% of those suffering hardships are women.

Both men and women long for love. For the flow of love to remain unbroken, it must be given continuously. If one side stops expressing love, sooner or later, the other side will also stop expressing it.

Both men and women have their weaknesses. But if we injure our left hand, won't the right hand caress it? Similarly, both women and men must patiently bear with each other's weaknesses. They must support each other. Unfortunately, ego and selfishness are now showing up where one ought to express love. This eventually leads to oppression and exploitation.

Men are physically stronger than women. That strength is not for oppressing women but protecting them. One might ask, if women need to be protected, does it not mean that they are weak? A protective ring of police officers surrounds the Prime

[17] Celebrated on March 8th every year.

Minister. Is it because he or she is weak? No, protecting the Prime Minister is in the interest of the country; it is the nation's duty. Similarly, protecting women is the duty of men and in their interest, too. Woman is the mother of man. Do not forget that every man was nourished by breast milk.

In many Indian villages, it is difficult to find grooms for uneducated women above 25 years of age. Without education, it is hard to find a job. As a result, these women suffer like unwelcome orphans for the rest of their life. Who is responsible for this? It is wrong to blame just men. Mothers must give their daughters equal opportunities in every field and equip them to become skilled enough to get a job.

Mothers should instill in their children from childhood the awareness that boys and girls are equal. Having been conditioned by mothers from a young age, women have forgotten their own strength. They have been raised like potted plants. They are like an eaglet reared by a hen. Deluded into thinking that it is also a chicken, the eaglet does not fly. Even its wings feel burdensome. Similarly, instead of fully allowing women to awaken their self-confidence, society has stymied their immense power. Many men behave as if women are beneath them. This will ultimately prove to be detrimental to men themselves, as they will not gain solace and inspiration from women.

Women and men are the two wings of society. Amma dreams of a bright future wherein both men and women play an equal part, like the two wings of a bird, in creating a better society. It is only through such equality that humankind can evolve.

Man and Woman

Children, all over the world, discussions are taking place on giving women equal rights at work and in other walks of life. This marks the beginning of change. For the longest time, in the absence of such discussions, women have suffered injustice silently. Women are discriminated against in many ways even in nations that claim to be progressive, developed and modern.

False pride and the egoistic belief that they are superior to women have become entrenched in men's minds. But women may think differently: "All this time, men controlled and oppressed us. They must be taught a lesson!" Women and men must stop competing to prove who is superior. As long as they do not accept and respect each other, their lives will be like the two separate banks of a river, unconnected by a bridge.

A wedding was taking place. When it came to signing the marriage register to make it legal, the husband signed first. And then as soon as the wife signed, the husband loudly proclaimed, "Over! This marriage is over! I want a divorce right now!"

Everyone was dumbstruck. The registrar asked, "Are you mad? What happened to provoke this reaction?"

The groom said, "What happened? Open your eyes and look! See my signature? How small and compact it is. Now look at her signature. How very long it is. Does anyone take up a whole page to sign? I know what this means. She will belittle me in life, too." Turning to the bride, he said, "Keep those ambitions to yourself! You'll never succeed in demeaning me!"

Right from the outset, most women and men start off on the wrong foot.

"Ever onward"—this seems to be the motto of women today. Indeed, they must progress. But, from time to time, they must also turn back to look at the child toddling behind. The mother must have some patience for the child's sake. It is not enough to give it space in the womb alone. She must also have some space for the child in her heart.

Women and men must support each other, understanding and accepting each other's strengths and limitations. The ideal way to win each other over is through humility and love. Only if women and men awaken equally and act can they usher in a new age of love, compassion and prosperity.

Protection of Women

Children, attacks against women have yet again come under the media spotlight. We see only the tip of the iceberg; the rest remains submerged in the ocean. Similar is the case with media coverage of these attacks.

We are careful while crossing a road with busy traffic. If we are not, we might meet with an accident. Women must be similarly cautious today. We must teach every child about the nature of the world, which is inhabited by people who might attack, exploit or behave rudely to them. We must teach our children how to respond appropriately to such people.

Youngsters these days want the liberty to interact freely with each other. In so doing, they will not hesitate to infringe on the boundary lines society has drawn, because they believe that doing so is progress. But progress is not about excessive freedom and the lack of responsibility. Similarly, safeguarding values is not suppression or tyranny. What we need is the kind of behavior we would naturally show our parents and siblings. At the same time, we must have situational awareness and exercise self-control. There needs to be a radical change in the way society thinks. Parents, teachers, the media, artists and writers play a crucial role in this regard. They must avoid sending the wrong message to society. They must convey the right message instead. There is a tendency in the media to depict women as objects of entertainment and to sensationalize attacks against them. We must wise up to the negative impact of such depictions.

In our society, both men and women have been equally 'conditioned.' An elephant can be securely tied to a small tree. Actually, it can easily uproot the tree and walk away, but because of the intimidation it received from childhood, it has forgotten its own strength and does not try to break free from captivity. To an extent, this is true of women also. For generations, men have enjoyed precedence over women and more authority than them. Therefore, they are unable to change according to the times. Both men and women must try to shed their 'conditioning' and do so at any cost.

Lust and anger are part of human nature. We must train our children to manage these emotions well. From childhood itself, both boys and girls must be given the right knowledge and values.

Our culture taught us to see women as mothers and girls as sisters. Let us reclaim that noble culture.

Freedom of Women

Children, men and women are not two separate entities, but two manifestations of the same truth. There is a woman in every man and a man in every woman. Therefore, they are equal. Their dharma (duties) is not mutually contradictory but complementary.

Man must not change society into a one-way road along which he alone can progress. Society must become a highway in which women also enjoy equal freedom to advance.

Some men act as if women are inferior to them. Such an attitude will prove detrimental to men because the hardships faced by women, who are also mothers, will affect their children. If women are discouraged, men will not receive the necessary encouragement, inspiration and help from them. The advancement of women is an advantage to men and vice versa. Neglecting women will lead to the downfall of men.

Amma remembers a story. A group of travelers were crossing a wooden bridge over a swiftly flowing river. Suddenly, the bridge broke. Four of the travelers caught hold of a rope. One of them was a woman. They clung to the rope for dear life in the hope that someone would rescue them soon. When they saw that the rope was breaking under their weight, they decided that one of them would have to jump into the river to prevent the rope from snapping. The men looked at the woman in silent expectation that she should jump into the river. She agreed. But before jumping, she delivered a glorious sermon on the greatness of sacrifice. When she had finished, the three men instinctively started clapping their hands. You can guess what happened next.

Mothers must remember one thing: they must instill in their children the awareness that both boys and girls are equal. They must give girls equal opportunity to participate in and be exposed to all spheres of activity and thus boost their self-confidence. Girls should be educated, just like boys, and be equipped with the skills needed to get a job. Then, there will be more mutual respect between boys and girls. This attitude will continue to prevail even when they grow up.

Both men and women must understand that excessive freedom does not bestow happiness. Husband and wife must be of one mind in unity and love. They must open up to each other. They must become each other's strength and inspiration. They must provide succor and support to each other and become a source of happiness to one another.

Know the Heart and Act

Children, if we want to see the dawn of peace and harmony in the world, we must begin at home. Ninety percent of the problems in family life are caused by unhealed wounds from the past. All of us live with many such unhealed wounds. The way to heal these wounds is for the wife and husband to open up to each other.

Some men do not have the patience to listen to anything the wife says. They regard women as weaklings. They believe that nothing a woman says is of any substance. This is not to say that women have no weaknesses. Some women give undue importance to silly matters and cry over them. Generally, women cannot contain their emotions. They express it. But men are largely different. They keep their emotions hidden. Instead of expecting women to be like them, men must cultivate the patience to listen to women when they express their feelings of pain and suffering. Do not see them merely as objects of pleasure or as servants. Their heart longs for love, too. So, instead of brushing them aside, men must find the time and patience to listen to them. If men are not willing to do this, women might look elsewhere to unburden their hearts.

Similarly, women must also be ready to understand the husband's heart and act accordingly. If not, he might look elsewhere to unburden his heart. Often, the husband returns home after a hard day at work, where he had to bear the brunt of his superior's anger. If the wife receives him with a sullen face and angry words, he will become even more upset. Therefore, she must try to understand his state of mind.

If both husband and wife work, they must console each other. Only if they open up to each other and express what they are feeling can problems be solved. When there is greater mutual love and trust, problems will decrease. Such love and trust form the foundation of a good family. Problems will increase if we reject this knowingly or unknowingly.

It is said that a woman ought to have three attitudes: that of a mother, a wife, and a friend. Similarly, a man has his own dharma also, and he must fulfil it.

Children, may you love each other and become one.

98. Express Love

Children, many women tell Amma, "When I tell my husband about my sorrows, he just grunts. He doesn't give me even a word of consolation. He also doesn't show me any love." When Amma asks the husbands about this, they say, "It's not so. I love my wife a lot. But all she does is complain!" So, even though both have love, neither is benefited by it. It is like living on the banks of a river and dying of thirst.

Actually, there is love within everyone. But love that is not expressed is like honey trapped in a rock. We will not be able to enjoy its sweetness.

As we do not know each other's heart, it is not enough to keep our love confined to the heart. We must express it through words and deeds. We must love openly and share our love with others.

Once, a sanyāsī visited a prison and exchanged pleasantries with the prison inmates. There was a juvenile delinquent among them. Seeing the fate that had befallen the boy, the sanyāsī's heart melted. He approached the boy, caressed his back gently and asked, "My child, how did you fall into the company of these criminals?" As he spoke, the eyes of the sanyāsī overflowed with tears.

Seeing this, the boy softly said, "If there had been someone to place loving hands on my shoulder when I was younger and speak words of affection to me, I would not have reached this place."

It is necessary to show children love. They must be trained to receive and give love.

Love is not meant be hidden in the heart but expressed in word, look and deed. Love is the wealth that gives more happiness to the giver than to the receiver. It is a kind of wealth that we are not aware of though we hold it in our hands.

Therefore, let us awaken our inner love. May it flow out to the world through our every look, word and deed. May it flow unimpeded by the walls of caste, creed or clan. May hearts embrace each other, awaken the joy within, and share that bliss with others. May the flow of love caress all beings. May our lives on earth thus become blessed.

99. Bond Between Husband and Wife

Children, in order to enjoy a happy married life, mutual understanding, goodwill and a willingness to compromise are essential. Only then can couples overcome the challenges that arise in their marriage. Family bonds are weakening in our country. Divorces are increasing by the day.

Both men and women must understand that, at the emotional level, they are quite different. Man lives in his brain, and woman, in her heart. More than anything, the wife longs for emotional support from her husband. She wants a husband who shows her love and attention, and who is ready to listen sympathetically to her. The husband longs for attention, acceptance, love and respect from his wife. If there is love, both will serve each other and find happiness in this.

To understand and trust each other while lovingly sustaining married life is not an easy task. It takes a lot of patience and tolerance. Often, people who get married are immature and unable to understand the thoughts and emotional needs of their partner. Love is not the physical attraction one feels for another. Real love is the union of souls.

Nowadays, many young men and women dream of the kind of married life they see on television or in the movies, and they become disappointed when they are unable to recreate it in their own lives. Amma remembers an incident. A young girl was mesmerized by a movie she saw before her marriage. The husband and wife in the movie were extremely rich. They had a big house, an expensive car, fashionable clothes and every other luxury. They were always happy. After seeing this movie, the girl began visualizing such a life for herself. Soon, she got married. But her husband held an ordinary job. The wife wanted a car and new saris, and wanted to go to the cinema daily. What could the poor husband do? The wife became sorely disappointed. They began fighting and both lost their peace of mind. Finally, they got divorced.

Young men and women must aim not only for a good education and career. Both must also prepare themselves mentally for a happy married life even before they get married. In matrimony, neither spouse has the right to make demands constantly. Both of them must be ready to love and co-operate with each other and wait patiently for their love and co-operation to be reciprocated. There will be many problems in each of their personal lives. When that happens, they must be a source of strength and solace for each other. This way, their love will grow naturally.

Love and sacrifice are the two wings of family life that help married couples fly into the skies of joy and contentment.

100. Sympathy and Compassion

Children, at first glance, sympathy and compassion seem alike, but if we look deeply, we will see that there is a world of difference between the two. Sympathy is a momentary feeling that passes through the mind on seeing the sorrowful plight of another person. This feeling neither touches one deeply nor influences one greatly. Seeing the other person's sorrow, one might extend a little help or speak a kind word in order to ease one's own anguish. Compassion, however, is a state in which one experiences the sorrow of another as one's own. There is no duality here, only identification and oneness. When the left hand is injured, the right hand will caress it because the pain belongs to the one, undivided whole.

Once, a disciple asked a Guru, "What is real compassion?"

The Guru took the disciple to a street near the āśram and asked him to observe carefully a beggar sitting by the wayside. After a while, a poor old woman passing by threw a coin into his begging bowl. Moments later, a wealthy man gave the beggar ₹50. Sometime later, a child came by and, seeing the beggar, smiled sweetly at him. The boy went near him and talked to the beggar as if he were his older brother. The beggar was touched and pleased. Turning to his disciple, the Guru asked, "Who among the three had real compassion?"

The disciple said, "The rich man."

Smiling, the Guru said, "He did not have an iota of sympathy or compassion for the beggar. His only intention was to make a show of his generosity. The old woman had sympathy for the beggar, though she did not see the beggar as her own or have an intense desire to alleviate his poverty. The child had compassion because he behaved as if the beggar was his own kin. Even though he was unable to help the beggar materially, there was empathy and a bonding of two hearts. What the boy demonstrated was real compassion."

What the world needs today is not fleeting sympathy but heartfelt compassion. Compassion dawns in the heart that sees the joys and sorrows of others as its own. Such hearts will be filled with love and a readiness to serve. Compassion is the only medicine that can heal the wounds of the world.

101. Compromise

Children, everyone dreams of a family life filled with love and unity. But everywhere today, we see families breaking up over trivial issues. Even if a handful of rice is all there is to eat at home, that home will be a heaven if it is filled with love and unity. In contrast, even if there is abundant money and wealth, a home will be a veritable hell if family members are constantly at loggerheads with each other.

Many fights happen over silly matters. Some women say, "My husband always says that he loves me a lot. How can I believe it when he doesn't even remember our wedding anniversary? I cannot forgive him for that. I don't wish to live with him!"

Many spouses have such complaints. Forgetting the date of the wedding anniversary might not reflect a lack of love. He might have forgotten for other reasons. In such situations, both sides must be willing to compromise.

A man sat down to eat breakfast with his son. As it was time for him to go to work, his wife quickly brought him *dōśa* (Indian pancake) and chutney. As the dōśa had been made hastily, most of it was burnt. Nevertheless, the man ate it without comment. Seeing this, his wife apologetically said, "That dōśa was burnt. Let me make you another."

The husband said "No, that's okay. This is crispy, and I love crispy dōśas!"

On his way to the office, the man drove his son to school. In the car, the son asked, "Dad, do you really like burnt dōśa?"

He said, "My dear son, your mother was on night duty yesterday. She was working the whole night and did not get any sleep. It was morning by the time she got home. She must have been really tired, and yet, she prepared breakfast for us. She has made us so many delicious breakfasts before but we've never told her how tasty the food was. Today, when she is so tired, if we had told her that the dōśa she made was burnt and refused to eat it because of that, she would have been hurt. I've no problems eating slightly burnt dōśa to make her feel happy."

We must realize that no one in this world is perfect. Love and peace in family life can be sustained only if there is mutual understanding between family members and an attitude of give and take.

102. Adjust to Circumstances

Children, change is the nature of life, and we must face different kinds of situations in life. We must learn to adjust to changing situations. While driving, we might encounter bumps, potholes, turns and uphill roads, and we shift gears accordingly. Similarly, whether at home or at work, we must adjust to changing circumstances. For example, even if we are angry with our superior or disagree with him on issues, we will smile and politely offer him a seat when he enters our office. Otherwise, we know that our job might be affected. Likewise, instead of trying to change objects and people to our liking, we must adapt to them.

One morning, while taking a walk in the palace premises, the king's foot accidentally hit a stone. Blood started oozing from the wound. The king was furious with his attendants. "Why didn't you clear this path, knowing full well that I was going to walk this way?" He ordered that all the roads in the city be carpeted before his morning walk the next day.

Hearing this, his ministers were dumbstruck. It was impossible to carpet all the roads in a day. They racked their brains on how to do this. Finally, an elderly minister had an idea. He humbly told the king, "Your majesty, instead of carpeting all the roads in the city, isn't it more practical for you to wear a good pair of shoes when you go for your morning walk?"

The eyes adjust themselves to changing scenes. The lens in the eyes adjusts according to whether the object is near or far. Similarly, we must acquire the ability to accommodate the ever-changing circumstances of life. If we can do this successfully, the world will become a heaven on earth for us.

In order to maintain equanimity amidst the vicissitudes of life, we must understand and assimilate spiritual principles. Spiritual knowledge is like the shock absorber in vehicles which helps to cushion the impact of traveling along rugged roads with bumps and potholes. Life also has highs and lows. If our outlook is firmly rooted in spiritual knowledge, we will be able to maintain our mental balance through all the vicissitudes of life.

103. Word and Deed

Children, we live in an age of talks and lectures taking place constantly throughout the country. What matters is not what is said or heard but the conviction of the speaker and the extent to which the listener assimilates what he or she hears.

Once, members of a temple committee invited a *mahātmā* (spiritually illumined soul) for a series of lectures as part of the temple festivities. The first talk was attended by 2,000 people, all of whom enjoyed the talk so much that they returned the next day to listen to him. But the mahātmā repeated what he had spoken the previous day. As a result, fewer people attended his talk on the third day. As the saint kept delivering the same lecture day after day, the numbers of those who came to hear him began to dwindle. By the end of the week, only a handful of people turned up to listen to him. On the eighth day, only a single devotee attended his talk, and on that day, the saint spoke on a new topic. When the lecture ended, the devotee asked the saint, "You spoke on the same subject all these days, but today, when I was the only person attending your talk, you started speaking on a new topic. Why?"

The mahātmā replied, "None of those who came to hear me speak applied the principles I spoke of in their lives. That's why I kept repeating the same points. But you assimilated two of the values I spoke about in your life. Yesterday, when a beggar came to your house to beg for clothes, you unhesitatingly gave him a set of your clothes even though you cannot afford to do so. Today when you came to the temple, the security officer scolded you for leaving your slippers in the wrong place. But you did not lose your composure. You calmly apologized and put your slippers in the right place. Thus, you have applied in your life the two values my talks stressed. When I felt assured that you were practicing what you heard, I started speaking on a new subject."

When the words we hear penetrate our heart deeply, they will create a change in us and reflect in our lives. Others will follow our example. Values transmitted in this way from one person to another will bring about a positive change in society as a whole.

104. In Search of Pleasure

Children, some people ask, "Isn't youth the time to enjoy the pleasures of life? Isn't it enough to think about God and *sanyāsa* (life of renunciation) when one is old?"

No one says that we should not enjoy the pleasures of life. But if we live without understanding certain truths of life, instead of finding happiness, we will find ourselves overwhelmed by sorrow. Actually, spirituality is nothing but the search for happiness. It is the wisest quest.

We unknowingly lose our strength while enjoying worldly pleasures, whereas our mind becomes filled with peace and happiness when we think about God. Therefore, we must strive to overcome our inner weaknesses while the body is still healthy. If we do so, we need not fear the future or worry in the present either.

Amma remembers a story. In a country, any citizen was entitled to become king. However, there were certain conditions attached. He could be king for five years only. After that, he would be exiled to a nearby island, which was inhabited by ferocious beasts. There were no humans there as the wild animals would devour anyone who came to the isle. Despite knowing this, many came forward to rule the country for five years, tempted by the prospect of royal pleasures and power.

Every new king would be happy initially but would soon be gripped by fear and anxiety, for he knew that after his five-year reign, wild animals would eat him up. His face would become permanently clouded by sorrow. He would not be enthusiastic about anything: the sumptuous food, the palatial opulence, the servants attending to his every need, or the constant flow of music and dance in the royal court. Nothing would hold any interest for him. When his reign ended, he would be taken to the island, where he would instantly be devoured by the wild animals.

Then came a young man, who wanted to be king. Unlike his predecessors, this new king did not show any sorrow. He looked into the welfare of his subjects, discharged his kingly duties ably, and spent his free time reveling in dance and music. He went horseback riding and hunting. He was always merry. Years passed and his reign began drawing to a close. Even then, there was no change in his demeanor. Everyone was amazed. They asked him, "Though the day you will be sent to the island is drawing near, you don't seem upset at all. What's your secret?"

The king said, "Why should I grieve? I'm prepared to go to the island. As soon as I became king, the first thing I did was to take the army to the island and clear it of the wild beasts. I also cleared part of the jungle and converted it into farmland. I had wells dug and houses built. I appointed workers. I resettled many people on the island. All I need to do now is to move there. Even though I am going to vacate the throne, I shall continue to live like a king on the island."

Children, we ought to live like this king. While living in the world, we must do whatever is necessary to find the way to eternal happiness. Worldly life can never give us lasting contentment. While drinking *pāyasam* (sweet pudding), we might feel satiated. But after a while, the craving for pāyasam will be twice as strong. Therefore, never think that we can seek God after enjoying worldly pleasures.

If we wish to overcome sorrow, we must strive to do so while the body and mind are still healthy. We must abandon the idea that we need to think about God only when we are old. Without postponing the search for God by even a day, we must do all our actions with the heart fixed firmly on God even from a young age. Let us engage in spiritual practices. Then, we can conquer death and always be happy.

105. Yearning

Children, devotion is supreme love for God. One must have the same burning desire to merge in God as someone trapped in a burning house and desperately trying to escape from the fire. Devotion gets fulfilled only when there is such an intensity. Some people ask, "God dwells in us. Why then do we need to have such intense longing?" Although God is within us, we are unable to feel His presence because our mind is chasing external objects. In order to tether such a mind to God, intense longing is certainly necessary. If a speck of dust gets into our eye, we will know no peace until the speck is removed. We must have such an all-consuming desire to attain God.

Once, Sage Nārada saw some priests looking despondent. When he asked them why they were sad, they said, "We have been performing *yajñas* (sacred fire rites) for many years but we've still not seen God."

Nārada said, "It's true that you have performed yajñas for years. But do you have innocent love for God? I know a fisherman who longed to see Dēvī. He went to his Guru, who advised him, 'If you call out to Dēvī with as much ardor as a man held under water longs for air, She will come to you.' The man had total faith in the Guru's words. With no thought whatsoever for his body, home or even life, he resolved, 'I'll come up for air only after I have seen Mother.' Calling out, 'Mother!' he submerged himself in water. Dēvī appeared before him immediately and asked, 'Son, why did you call me? What do you want?' The fisherman said, 'I don't need anything. I just wanted to see You. O Mother, please bless the world. And whenever You feel hungry, please come to my home to have some food.'" Nārada continued, "Call out to God with the same love and innocent longing like the fisherman. God will certainly appear before you."

God and the *jīva* (individual self) are not separate. Like a drop of water that longs to merge in the ocean, every jīva has the inner longing to become one with God. But such longing is dormant at the moment. Through the constant remembrance of God and actions dedicated to him, we can awaken that love and longing.

We must reach a state wherein we feel that we cannot live without God anymore. Once we gain such an intense longing, life will become fulfilled.

106. Inner Strength

Children, problems and challenges are an inevitable part of human life. We might falter when we come face to face with problems or give in to despair or fear. But we should never forget that we possess the inner strength to overcome unfavorable circumstances. We can awaken that power through optimistic faith and a never-say-die attitude.

Once, a frog fell into a hole while hopping along a road. It tried hard to get out but failed. A rabbit passing that way saw the frog's predicament and its heart melted in pity. It tried to help the frog but failed. The rabbit called its friends, who also tried to get the frog out. But their attempts also failed. By then, they were exhausted and hungry. They said, "We'll have something to eat and come back with food for you. Please wait patiently until then." Saying so, they left. They had gone only a little distance when they saw, to their amazement, the frog hopping ahead of them! In one voice, the rabbits asked, "How did you come out so quickly?"

The frog said, "I was feeling despondent, thinking that I would never be able to get out. That's when I saw a truck hurtling towards me. With no further thought, I leaped, and here I am!"

We must see the problems arising in life as circumstances arranged by God to rouse our inner strength. When our foot is pricked by a small thorn, we will walk with more awareness and thus be saved from falling into a big pit.

If we continue lifting only small weights, we can never become a champion weightlifter. To become a champion, we must gradually increase the weights we lift. We might start by lifting a 25-kilogram disc. We must then increase the weight we lift to 30 kg, 40 kg, 50 kg and so on. Only if we consistently train this way can we excel in any field.

Problems and crises are just means to discover and awaken our inner strength. We must accept every challenge with this understanding. Where there is hope and effort, victory is assured. We must never give up hope.

107. Love Yourself

Children, we live in an age where we hate not only others but also ourselves. That is why cases of depression and suicides are on the rise. All religions, spiritual masters and psychologists throughout the world teach the importance of loving oneself just as we love others.

Generally, people think that loving themselves means pampering the body. Some spend hours in front of the mirror upon waking up. Many invest heavily in maintaining their physical beauty and health. They have no qualms spending time and money bleaching dark skin, tanning fair skin, dyeing white hair or coloring black hair. No one even considers this a waste. But they do not give as much attention to honing their intelligence.

There was a multi-storied supermarket with not enough elevators. Customers had to wait a long time. Fed up with waiting, they started complaining loudly. The manager realized that if he did not resolve this problem immediately, business would be adversely affected. He considered various solutions and finally found one. He installed mirrors at the elevator lobby and inside the elevator. After that, there were no complaints. The people waiting for the elevators did not notice time passing as they were busy combing their hair, powdering their faces, and applying lipstick or eyeliner, which they continued doing even after entering the elevator.

Just as we take the trouble to keep the body clean and looking good, we must make efforts to hold negative thoughts and emotions at bay, thus keeping our mind clean. Similarly, we must train the intellect to think discerningly by exposing the mind to knowledge that will help us do so. In this way, we can unveil the inner divinity. This is what loving oneself really means.

108. Controlling the Mind

Children, it is the mind that makes life a heaven or hell. Therefore, anyone who desires his or her own good must control the mind. Two things are needed for this: patient effort and unflagging enthusiasm. That said, we should not apply too much pressure on the mind. We must not overly control the body's basic needs such as food and sleep. If we exert undue pressure on the mind, it will become agitated. We must control it gradually. We must give both body and mind enough opportunities for rest and recreation. At the same time, we must continue to put forth as much effort as we can in order to reach the goal. It is not easy to control the mind. We might fail. Even so, we must keep trying without losing heart.

Suppose we feel a strong urge to urinate while traveling in a bus. We will somehow control ourselves until the next stop. We will not jump out of a moving bus. Likewise, if the mind prompts us to do wrong for the sake of fleeting pleasure, we must not give in. We must reflect and discriminate, and thus control the mind. Through constant practice, the mind will come under our control.

Some argue that there is no point in controlling emotions like anger and lust. They say that lust is a kind of hunger that must be appeased. However, no matter how hungry we are, we will not gobble down everything we see in front of us. Similarly, even though anger and lust are natural emotions, we must be careful not to give them free rein. We can bring them under our control, and such control is necessary for the benefit of both the individual and society.

What gives us strength to overcome obstacles is focus on the goal. A student who earnestly longs to score the highest marks on an examination will set and follow a routine. He knows that if he stays up late to watch TV, he will not be able to wake up early. So, he will curtail the time spent watching TV. Similarly, he knows that if he eats a heavy meal at night, he will find it difficult to wake up early to study. Taking such factors into consideration, he will draw up a timetable for himself. He will be careful not to eat, sleep, play or talk too much. Similarly, one who is strongly driven to attain his goal will definitely succeed in bringing his mind under control.

Listening to spiritual discourses and cultivating the company of noble people will increase our will power. Spiritual practices such as meditation and *japa* (repeated chanting of the mantra) will calm and strengthen the mind, and enable us to gain control of the mind easily.

Glossary

adharma: unrighteousness; deviation from natural harmony.

Arjuna: great archer and one of the heroes of the *Mahābhārata*. It is Arjuna whom Kṛṣṇa addresses in the *Bhagavad-Gītā*.

artha: goal, wealth, substance; one of the four *puruṣārthas* (goals of human endeavor).

āśram: monastery. Amma defines it as a compound: '*ā*'—'that' and '*śramam*'—'effort' (toward Self-realization).

Bhagavad-Gītā: 'Song of the Lord,' it consists of 18 chapters of verses in which Lord Kṛṣṇa advises Arjuna. The advice is given on the battlefield of Kurukṣētra, just before the righteous Pāṇḍavas fight the unrighteous Kauravas. It is a practical guide to overcoming crises in all areas of life and is the essence of Vedic wisdom.

bhajan: devotional song or hymn in praise of God.

bhakti: devotion for God.

Bhārat: India.

Bharata: Rāma's younger brother; he ruled Ayōdhya as Rāma's representative while the latter was in exile.

bhaya-bhakti: devotion inspired by fear of the repercussions of wrongdoing.

Bhīma: one of the Pāṇḍava brothers; a warrior of Herculean strength; the target of many of Duryōdhana's sadistic attacks.

Bhīṣma: patriarch of the Pāṇḍava and Kaurava clan. Though he fought on the side of the Kauravas during the Mahābhārata War, he championed dharma and was sympathetic to the righteous Pāṇḍavas.

darśan: audience with a holy person or a vision of the Divine. Amma's signature darśan is a hug.

Daśaratha: Father of Rāma and king of Kōśala.

Dēvī: Goddess / Divine Mother.

dharma: 'that which upholds (creation).' It refers to the harmony of the universe, a righteous code of conduct, sacred duty or eternal law.

dharmakṣētra: 'field of dharma (righteousness);' a reference to the battlefield in which the Mahābhārata War was fought.

Dhṛtarāṣṭra: father of the Kauravas.

Drōṇa: teacher of both the Pāṇḍavas and Kauravas in the *Mahābhārata.*

Duryōdhana: eldest of the Kauravas; the embodiment of evil.

Gaṇapati: elephant-headed son of Śiva; invoked as the remover of obstacles.

Gāndhārī: mother of the Kauravas; as an expression of solidarity with her blind husband, Dhṛtarāṣṭra, she blindfolded herself after marriage.

gōpa: cowherd boy from Vṛndāvan.

gōpī: milk maiden from Vṛndāvan. The gōpīs were known for their ardent devotion to Lord Kṛṣṇa. Their devotion exemplifies the most intense love for God.

Guru: spiritual teacher.

Gurukula: literally, the clan (*kula*) of the preceptor (*Guru*); traditional school where students would stay with the Guru for the entire duration of their scriptural studies.

Hanumān: the *vānara* (monkey) disciple and companion of Rāma and one of the key characters in the *Rāmāyaṇa*.

hōma: ancient Vēdic fire ritual in which oblations are offered to the gods by offering ghee into a consecrated fire; a *dēva-yajña*, one of the five daily *yajñas* to be performed by a Brāhmin.

iṣṭa dēvata: preferred form of divinity.

japa: repeated chanting of a mantra.

jīva (jīvātmā): individual self or soul.

Kaikēyī: second wife of Daśaratha and mother of Bharata (in the *Rāmāyaṇa*).

kalpavṛkṣa: mythical wish-fulfilling tree.

kāma: desire.

Kamsa: Kṛṣṇa's maternal uncle.

karma: action; mental, verbal and physical activity; chain of effects produced by our actions.

karma-yōga: the way of action, the path of selfless service.

Karṇa: son of the sun-god and Kuntī, the mother of the Pāṇḍavas. Karṇa fought on the side of the Kauravas in the Mahābhārata War.

Kauravas: the 101 children of King Dhṛtarāṣṭra and Queen Gāndhārī, of whom the unrighteous Duryōdhana was the eldest. The Kauravas were the enemies of their cousins, the virtuous Pāṇḍavas, whom they fought against in the Mahābhārata War.

Kṛṣṇa: from '*kṛṣ,*' meaning 'to draw to oneself' or 'to remove sin;' principal incarnation of Lord Viṣṇu. He was born into a royal family but raised by foster parents, and lived as a cowherd boy in Vṛndāvan, where he was loved and worshipped by his devoted companions, the *gōpīs* (milkmaids) and *gōpas* (cowherd boys). Kṛṣṇa later established the city of Dwāraka. He was a friend and advisor to his cousins, the Pāṇḍavas, especially Arjuna, whom he served as charioteer during the Mahābhārata War, and to whom he revealed his teachings as the *Bhagavad-Gītā*.

Kṣatriya: ruler or warrior; one of the four *varṇas* (social order) of ancient Hindu society.

Kucēla: A poor devotee of Lord Kṛṣṇa. As a result of the Lord's blessings, he became fabulously wealthy.

Kurukṣētra: battlefield where the war between the Pāṇḍavas and Kauravas was fought; also, a metaphor for the conflict between good and evil.

Lakṣmaṇa: younger brother of Rāma.

lakṣya-bōdha: goal-orientedness.

Mahābalī: a kind, generous and just ruler who became famed for his utopian rule.

Mahābhārata: ancient Indian epic that Sage Vyāsa composed, depicting the war between the righteous Pāṇḍavas and the unrighteous Kauravas.

mahātmā: 'great soul;' term used to describe one who has attained spiritual realization.

mānasa-pūjā: worship done mentally.

mantra: a sound, syllable, word or words of spiritual content. According to Vēdic commentators, mantras are revelations of ṛṣis arising from deep contemplation.

mōkṣa: spiritual liberation, i.e. release from the cycle of births and deaths.

niyama: positive duties or observances (the 'do's'); the second 'limb' of the *aṣṭāṅga yōga* (eight limbs) formulated by Sage Patañjali, and they include *śauca* (purity), *santōṣa* (contentment), *tapas* (austerity), *swādhyāya* (scriptural study) and *īśvara-praṇidhāna* (contemplation of God); often mentioned in association with *yama.*

Ōm (Aum): primordial sound in the universe; the seed of creation. The cosmic sound, which can be heard in deep meditation; the Holy Word, taught in the Upaniṣads, which signifies Brahman, the divine ground of existence.

Ōṇam: Kerala's biggest festival, occurring in the month of *Ciṅṅam* (August – September).

Pāṇḍavas: five sons of King Pāṇḍu, and cousins of Kṛṣṇa.

paramātmā: supreme self, the oversoul.

pāyasam: sweet pudding.

praṇava: the mystic syllable *'Ōm.'*

prārabdha: also known as *prārabdha karma*; refers to the part of our past karma that is the cause of our present birth.

prasād: blessed offering or gift from a holy person or temple, often in the form of food.

prasāda-buddhi: the attitude of seeing everything one receives as a gift from God.

pūjā: ritualistic or ceremonial worship.

puṇya: spiritual merit.

Rāma: divine hero of the *Rāmāyaṇa.* An incarnation of Lord Viṣṇu, he is considered the ideal man of *dharma* and virtue. *'Ram'* means 'to revel;' one who revels in himself; the principle of joy within; one who gladdens the hearts of others.

Rāma-rajya: literally, 'rule of Rāma.' The term has come to mean a utopian age.

Rāmāyaṇa: 24,000-verse epic poem on the life and times of Rāma.

Rāvaṇa: powerful demon. Viṣṇu incarnated as Lord Rāma to kill him and thereby restore harmony to the world.

ṛṣi: Self-realized seer or sage who also perceive mantras in their meditation.

Śabarī: devotee of Rāma known for her unflagging faith.

Śabarimala: location of the Śabarimala Temple, dedicated to Lord Ayyappa.

sādhana: regimen of disciplined and dedicated spiritual practice that leads to the supreme goal of Self-realization.

Śalya: King of Madra and great warrior. At Yudhiṣṭhira's request, he served as Karṇa's charioteer with a view to demoralizing the latter at critical moments in the Mahābhārata War.

samskāra: a personality trait conditioned over one or many lives: a mental and behavioral pattern; a latency or tendency within the mind which will manifest itself if given the proper environment or stimulus.

Sanātana Dharma: literally, 'Eternal Religion' or 'Eternal Way of Life,' the original and traditional name of Hinduism.

Sañjaya: narrator of the *Bhagavad-Gītā* and character from the *Mahābhārata* on whom Sage Vyāsa bestowed the gift of *divya-dṛṣṭi* (clairvoyance) so that he could relate the happenings on the battlefield to King Dhṛtarāṣṭra.

sannyāsī: monk who has taken formal vows of renunciation (*sannyāsa*); traditionally wears an ocher-colored robe, representing the burning away of all desires. The female equivalent is ***sannyāsinī***.

satsaṅg: communion with the Supreme Truth. Also, being in the company of *mahātmās*, studying the scriptures, and listening to the enlightening talks of a mahātmā; a meeting of people to listen to and/or discuss spiritual matters; a spiritual discourse.

Sītā: Rāma's consort. In India, she is considered to be the ideal of womanhood.

Śiva: worshipped as the first and the foremost in the lineage of Gurus and as the formless substratum of the universe in relationship to Śakti, the creatrix; Lord of destruction (of the ego) in the Hindu Trinity.

śraddhā: attentiveness; faith.

Swāmī Vivēkānanda: chief disciple (1863 – 1902) of Śrī Rāmakṛṣṇa Paramahamsa, a pioneer in introducing Hindu philosophy to the West, and founder of the Ramakrishna Math and Ramakrishna Mission.

upāsanā: worship.

vāsanā: latent tendency or subtle desire that manifests as thought, motive and action; subconscious impression gained from experience.

vasudhaiva kuṭumbakam: 'the world is one family.'

Vēdas: most ancient of all scriptures, originating from God, the Vēdas were not composed by any human author but were 'revealed' in deep meditation to the ancient seers. These sagely revelations came to be known as the Vēdas, of which there are four: *Ṛk*, *Yajus*, *Sāma* and *Atharva.*

Vyāsa: literally 'compiler.' The name given to Sage Kṛṣṇa Dvaipāyana, who compiled the Vēdas. He is also the chronicler of the *Mahābhārata* and a character in it, and author of the 18 Purāṇas and the *Brahma-Sūtras.*

yajña: form of ritual worship in which oblations are offered into a fire according to scriptural injunctions, while sacred mantras are chanted.

yama: restraints for proper conduct (the 'don'ts'); the first 'limb' of the *aṣṭānga yōga* (eight limbs) formulated by Sage Patanjali, and they include *ahimsā* (non-violence), *satya* (truthfulness), *astēya* (non-stealing), *brahmacarya* (chastity) and *aparigraha* (non-covetousness); often mentioned in association with *niyama.*

yōga: 'to unite.' Union with the Supreme Being. A broad term, it also refers to the various methods of practices through which one can attain oneness with the Divine. A path that leads to Self-realization.

yuddha: war.

Pronunciation Guide

Vowels can be short or long:
a – as 'u' in but; ā – as 'a' in far
e – as 'a' in may; ē – as 'a' in name
i – as 'i' in pin; ī – as 'ee' in meet
o – as in oh; ō – as 'o' in mole
u – as 'u' in push; ū – as 'oo' in hoot

ṛ – as ri in crisp
ḥ – pronounce 'aḥ' like 'aha,' 'iḥ' like 'ihi,' and 'uḥ' like 'uhu.'

Some consonants are aspirated (e.g. kh); others are not (e.g. k). The examples given below are only approximate:
k – as 'k' in 'kite;' kh – as 'ckh' in 'Eckhart'
g – as 'g' in 'give;' gh – as 'g-h' in 'dig-hard'
c – as 'c' in 'cello;' ch – as 'ch-h' in 'staunch-heart'
j – as 'j' in 'joy;' jh – as 'dgeh' in 'hedgehog'
p – as 'p' in 'pine;' ph – as 'ph' in 'up-hill'
b – as 'b' in 'bird;' bh – as 'bh' in 'rub-hard'

r – as 'r' in ride
ñ – as 'ny' in 'canyon;' ṅ – as 'ng' in 'sing'

The letters ḍ, ṭ, ṇ are pronounced with the tip of the tongue against the hard palate, the others with the tip against the teeth.
ṭ – as 't' in 'tub;' ṭh – as 'th' in 'lighthouse'
ḍ – as 'd' in 'dove;' ḍh – as 'dh' in 'red-hot'
ṇ – as 'n' in 'naught'
ḷ – as 'l' in 'revelry'
ṣ – as 'sh' in 'shine;' ś – as 's' in German 'sprechen'

With double consonants the sound is pronounced twice:
cc – as 'tc' in 'hot chip'
jj – as 'dj' in 'red jet'

www.ingramcontent.com/pod-product-compliance
Lightning Source LLC
Chambersburg PA
CBHW071210090426
42736CB00014B/2769
9781680378764